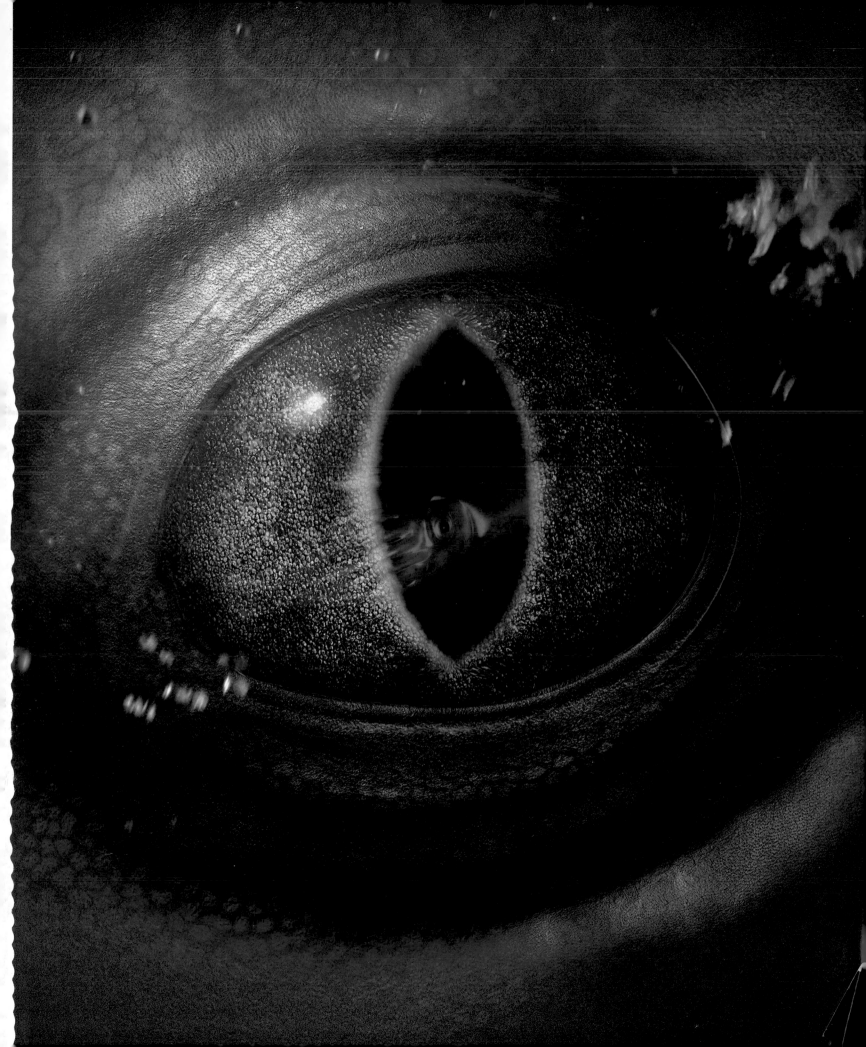

SEA MONSTERS

PREHISTORIC CREATURES OF THE DEEP

MIKE EVERHART

NATIONAL GEOGRAPHIC

WASHINGTON, D.C.

ABOVE: *This long-necked* Styosaurus *swam the Earth's seas over 82 million years ago.*

Getting this close to a
Tylosaurus could be deadly.
These creatures were among
the largest and most
successful predators of the
great marine reptiles.

CONTENTS

FOREWORD

DINOSAURS HAVE LONG had a monopoly on the public imagination. The meat-eating *T-Rex* and the strangely armored *Stegosaurus* leap easily to mind when thinking of the Mesozoic era, popularly called the "Age of the Dinosaurs." But at the same time, the oceans of the Earth were dominated by another group of fascinating yet often overlooked creatures: monstrous marine reptiles that ruled the oceans and seas just as the dinosaurs ruled the land. Everyone has heard of the *Tyrannosaurus*, but how many people know about the *Tylosaurus*?

While the first fossils of marine reptiles were discovered in The Netherlands and England decades before the word "Dinosauria" was coined by Richard Owen in 1842, they have received relatively little attention over the years. Modern vertebrate paleontology textbooks often have several chapters on dinosaurs, but marine reptiles seldom get more than a few pages. Mosasaurs, arguably the most successful sea monsters of all time, typically receive a few paragraphs or are often ignored altogether. This lack of knowledge was something that I sought to correct.

I've been interested in fossils and ancient life for about as long as I can remember. It wasn't until my first paleontology course in college, however, that I was introduced to the Smoky Hill chalk in Kansas, one of the world's best sources of Late Cretaceous marine fossils. Although my first specimens were limited to fragments of a small fish skull and a shark tooth, I was hooked. Several years later I collected my first mosasaur and became fascinated with these large, very successful, but little known marine predators. The more I learned about them, the more interested I became in exploring their world and telling people about them. Some mosasaurs were larger than *T-rex*, they were certainly more numerous and probably much more dangerous predators in their marine environment.

When work on the *Sea Monsters* movie began several years ago, I came on as an expert adviser. The aim for this new, exciting project was to create a dramatic film—one that would focus on the massive marine creatures who lived during the Mesozoic and introduce them to the general public. Unlike the December 2005 NATIONAL GEOGRAPHIC cover story on "Sea Monsters" (which covered a range of monsters from the Triassic, Jurassic, and Cretaceous periods), this movie would zero in on the Late Cretaceous period, about 82 million years ago. Through computer animation, the film follows the life and adventures of a *Dolichorhynchops* and the fascinating (and sometimes deadly) creatures she encounters. Live-action re-creations of paleontological digs are woven into the story to illustrate what we know about the sea monsters' world.

As one of the film's consultants, I spent many hours working with the Giant Screen Film's team to create the movie. Although I have participated in making documentaries before, this was my first time being involved in making a movie, and it was definitely an educational experience. A tremendous amount of research and hard work went into making the film both entertaining and accurate. While I am familiar with these creatures and have a good idea of what they might look like, explaining their appearance to others who knew little about them forced me to come up with better ways to explain them. It was both a teaching and a learning experience. As a result, I came away with a much better understanding of these sea monsters. Being an expert advisor on the animation process was painstaking yet extremely gratifying, as we were ultimately rewarded when these marine reptiles came to life.

This official companion book complements the fast-paced, dramatic 3-D movie. In it, the audience can find even more information about the sea monsters, their world, and the paleontologists who first discovered them. The breathtaking, computer-generated imagery from the movie appears throughout the book, and at the end of each chapter is a 3-D IMAGE GALLERY with dynamic shots taken straight from the movie (special 3-D glasses can be found inside the back cover). Each chapter features CLOSER LOOK sidebars on current scientific topics, and multi-paged PHOTO ALBUMS, many with never-before published photographs of historic specimens and the people who collected them. Throughout the book, there are many WEBLINKS to the official Sea Monsters website—http://nationalgeographic.com/seamonsters— for an interactive experience with the creatures from the movie. Creature profiles, virtual excavations, plus timelines and maps enhance the information in this book and the movie, giving even more science and information on all the sea monsters.

This book is an excellent written source of information on these strange and wonderful marine creatures, whose existence might make you think twice about what might be lurking in the water. I hope you enjoy this book as much as I enjoyed being a part of this project.

—Mike Everhart
Sternberg Museum of Natural History, Hays, Kansas

NOTHOSAURUS
GIGANTEUS
Order: *Nothosauria*
Jurassic Period • Europe
13 feet

WHAT IS A SEA MONSTER?

CHAPTER ONE

Ferocious teeth populated the mouth of the 13-foot-long Nothosaurus giganteus, *one of the earliest sea monster ancestors.*

T HE IDEA THAT THERE MIGHT BE UNKNOWN CREATURES OR "sea monsters" inhabiting the oceans of the Earth has been around for centuries, probably from the time that wooden ships were first built and sailed out of sight of land. In those days when people knew little about the land around them and less about the seas that surrounded the land, the ocean was a vast unknown. Put yourself in the shoes of one of the first sailors to venture far from shore, and then imagine your thoughts and fears at seeing a giant blue whale surfacing for the first time, without any prior knowledge that such creatures existed. What would be your reaction? What if you only saw part of the animal, for only a second or two, or as the sun was going down and light was fading? What sort of a creature would you believe this giant animal to be? How would you describe it to your family and friends, who had stayed safely on shore? Would you tell them it was a monster? A sea monster?

TEMNODONTOSAURUS
PLATYODON

Order: *Ichthyosauria*

Jurassic Period • Europe

30 feet

LEFT: *A* Temnodontosaurus, *its eyes 10 inches wide, considers squid-like belemnites as its prey. This type of ichthyosaur was capable of sight in near-lightless conditions and probably dove in search of food.*

SEA MONSTER EVOLUTION

Over millions of years, a wide variety of sea monsters evolved.

NOTHOSAURUS GIGANTEUS
230 M.Y.A.
Europe
13 feet
This creature is the earliest known sea monster ancestor.

SHONISAURUS SIKANNIENSIS
220–210 M.Y.A.
North America
75 feet
Discovered in Canada, remains of this ichthyosaur suggest it was the largest marine reptile ever.

TEMNODONTOSAURUS PLATYODON
195–175 M.Y.A.
Europe
30 feet
This creature had eyes the size of dinner plates, which helped it to hunt in deep, dark waters.

LIOPLEURODON FEROX
160–155 M.Y.A.
Europe
50 feet
A large pliosaur with powerful jaws and sharp teeth, it was at the top of the food chain.

150 million years ago

250
240
230
220
210
200
190
180
170
160

TRIASSIC PERIOD 251 MILLION TO 199 MILLION YEARS AGO

JURASSIC PERIOD 199 MILLION TO 145 MILLION YEARS AGO

Women stretch to gauge the size of a 200-million-year-old ichthyosaur from southern

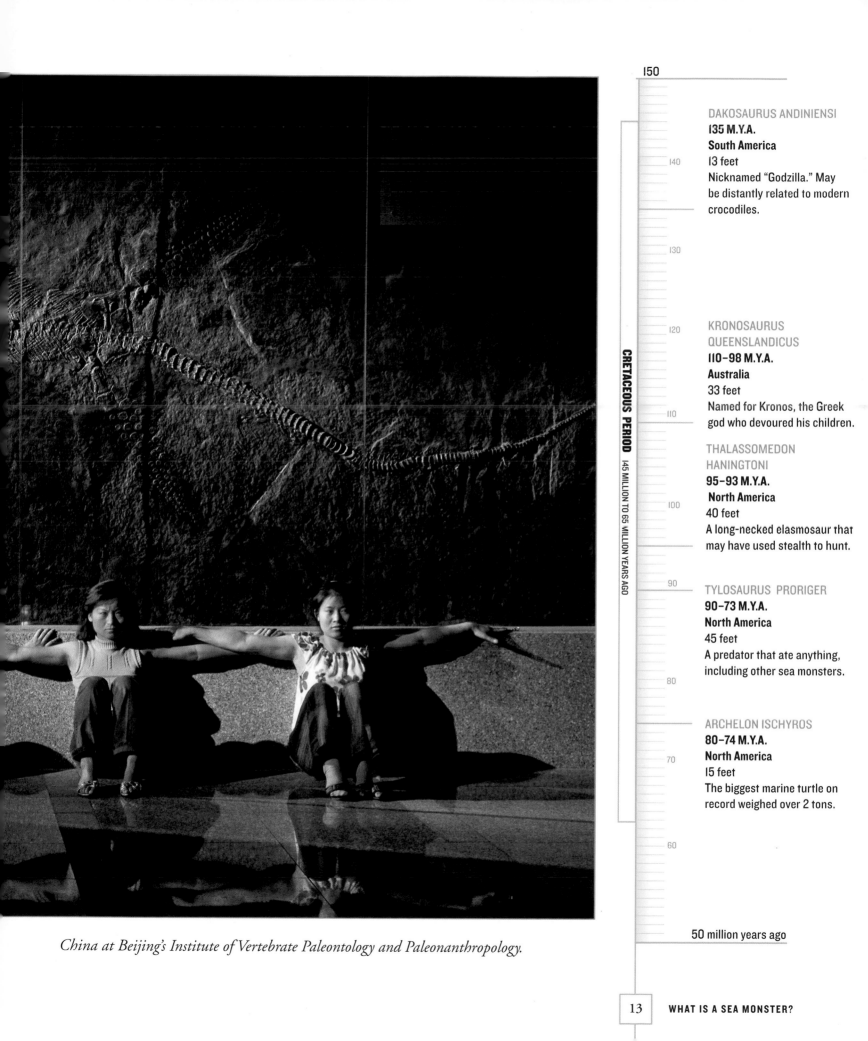

China at Beijing's Institute of Vertebrate Paleontology and Paleonanthropology.

150

140

DAKOSAURUS ANDINIENSI
135 M.Y.A.
South America
13 feet
Nicknamed "Godzilla." May be distantly related to modern crocodiles.

130

120

KRONOSAURUS QUEENSLANDICUS
110–98 M.Y.A.
Australia
33 feet
Named for Kronos, the Greek god who devoured his children.

110

THALASSOMEDON HANINGTONI
95–93 M.Y.A.
North America
40 feet
A long-necked elasmosaur that may have used stealth to hunt.

100

90

TYLOSAURUS PRORIGER
90–73 M.Y.A.
North America
45 feet
A predator that ate anything, including other sea monsters.

80

ARCHELON ISCHYROS
80–74 M.Y.A.
North America
15 feet
The biggest marine turtle on record weighed over 2 tons.

70

60

50 million years ago

CRETACEOUS PERIOD 145 MILLION TO 65 MILLION YEARS AGO

It seems fairly obvious that the early sailors on the oceans of the Earth believed exactly that about many of the unknown and unusual marine animals that they observed in the vastness of the oceans, and they shared their stories with others, including those who made the maps of the known world. It was a common practice for mapmakers (cartographers) to decorate the otherwise blank blue spaces that indicated the vast oceans on their maps with their imaginative ideas of the creatures that might live there. The earliest known map of Scandinavia (the Carta Marina, dated 1539) shows at least a dozen different strange creatures inhabiting the North Atlantic between Norway and Iceland, any of which could easily be considered a sea monster. It seems likely that

NOTHOSAURUS GIGANTEUS

Order: *Nothosauria*

Triassic Period • Europe

13 feet

these creatures were part fact and part fiction, with a large dose of the original observer's imagination thrown in for good measure.

Although there are numerous stories and even current sightings of the strange creatures that inhabit the sea, none seem to be truly bizarre and unknown sea monsters. Many of these sightings can eventually be identified as modern creatures which are known to science and sailors alike, whales, basking sharks, giant squid, and so forth, and many will never be identified. It does appear, however, that we do want to believe in sea monsters of one kind or another.

With that in mind, this book is about a time when real sea monsters inhabited the oceans of the Earth. That time was during the Mesozoic era, the so-called Age of Dinosaurs, 251 to 65 million years ago, when giant, meat-eating terrestrial reptiles ruled the land, and equally large and dangerous marine reptiles ruled the seas. The bones of these strange marine creatures were discovered in continental Europe and England long before the first remains of dinosaurs were collected, and well before the word "dinosaur" even existed. About 1760, the first specimens of these marine reptiles, mosasaurs, were first discovered in Late Cretaceous limestones of The Netherlands. Their discovery was followed quickly by those of ichthyosaurs and plesiosaurs in the Jurassic rocks of England. Based on their strange skeletons, the scientific publications of the day often showed imaginative drawings of what these prehistoric animals might have looked like and how they behaved. Even some early fiction writers (Jules Verne, for one, in his *Journey to the Center of the Earth*) used them to test their heroes and liven up their plots. More recently, our discoveries of better specimens of ichthyosaurs, plesiosaurs, and mosasaurs suggest that some of these marine predators were even larger than the largest known meat-eating dinosaurs (e.g., theropods like *Tyrannosaurus rex*, *Carcharodontosaurus saharicus*, etc.). For this and other reasons, we probably should have referred to the Mesozoic as the Age of Marine Reptiles (or even the Age of Sea Monsters).

WHAT IS A SEA MONSTER?

Okay then, what is a real sea monster? We can start by saying that it is not a big bony fish, or a large shark, or a pterosaur, and it is certainly *not* a dinosaur. That being said, we are left with several distinct kinds of large reptiles that lived in the oceans during the Age of Dinosaurs and were very well qualified to be called "sea monsters." At the same time as dinosaurs were evolving during the Mesozoic era, there were four major groups of reptiles that successfully left the land and returned to the sea. These were the

ichthyosaurs, the plesiosaurs, the marine turtles, and the mosasaurs. Other groups (like early marine crocodiles and placodonts) also adapted to life in the sea but were not nearly as successful or deserving of the title "sea monsters." It is important to note here that all of these marine reptiles are "air-breathers" and do not have gills like fish. They lived near the surface and had to come up periodically for air.

The ancestors of ichthyosaurs (literally "fish-lizards," or reptiles that were shaped very much like sharks, killer whales, and porpoises) were probably the first of our four groups to venture from the land to the sea. Remains from the Triassic period found in China, Japan, and elsewhere indicate

BELOW: *Miniature marine reptiles measured no longer than a human hand. These fossils of* Keichousaurus hui *were found in China's Guizhou Province.*

Since the fossil record preserves clusters of giant ichthyosaurs, paleontologists believe that they may have traveled the vast open waters in pods, as do modern whales.

that the first ichthyosaurs were small, rather long and sinuous, and not particularly fish-like in shape. They grew in size, perfected their fluke-like tail, and diversified rapidly. By the end of the Triassic period, there were some truly giant species of ichthyosaurs such as the 50-foot-long *Shonisaurus* remains found in Nevada, and even larger ones with skulls about 9 feet long that were discovered recently in Canada. The ichthyosaurs evolved into many different forms during the Triassic and Jurassic periods, and have been found in many places around the world. Preserved stomach contents show that they fed mostly on the small cephalopods (squid and belemnites) that were abundant at the time and even on small turtles and birds during their last days in the Early Cretaceous. Exquisitely preserved remains preserved in the black shales of Germany showed that ichthyosaurs gave live birth to their young, an adaptation to life in the ocean that appears to be essential to becoming a truly great sea monster. As large, diverse, and as well-adapted to life in the sea as they were, however, for unknown reasons the ichthyosaurs declined in numbers and diversity during the Late Jurassic, and then became extinct during the Early Cretaceous.

Plesiosaurs ("near-to lizards") were the second group of terrestrial reptiles to return to the sea. Fossils indicate that the earliest plesiosaurs probably entered the oceans during the Late Triassic. Little is known for certain about their ancestors, other than they appear to have been something like the aquatic lizards called nothosaurs that are common in some Triassic rocks. Although still relatively small, the early plesiosaurs had a flattened, oval-shaped body, and a small head on the end of a moderately long neck. They swam by using their four large, paddle-shaped limbs to generate thrust and allow them to literally "fly" through the water. A late-Cretaceous specimen of a short-necked plesiosaur from Kansas suggests that they also bore live young like the ichthyosaurs. Plesiosaurs evolved rapidly during the Jurassic into many species and are represented there by long-necked, small-headed varieties (true "plesiosaurs") and massive, short-necked, big-headed varieties that we call pliosaurs. Two species of pliosaurs found in the Jurassic rocks of England and Europe (*Pliosaurus* and *Liopleurodon*) are certainly among the largest marine reptiles ever. Other giant pliosaurs (*Kronosaurus* and *Brachauchenius*) were the biggest predators in the oceans of the Earth during the early years of the Late Cretaceous. Bite marks and evidence of crushing injuries on the bones of smaller plesiosaurs suggests that the larger pliosaurs preyed on them and probably anything else they wanted to eat.

Plesiosaurs suffered and survived several partial extinctions during the Mesozoic era. Several groups including the last of the giant pliosaurs were gone for good by the early part of the Late Cretaceous period. The remaining plesiosaurs were limited to the very long-necked elasmosaurs like *Styxosaurus* and *Elasmosaurus*, and their short-necked, small-headed cousins (polycotylids) like *Trinacromerum* and *Dolichorhynchops*. Fossils of both of these later occurring groups are never numerous, but they are found in many places around the world. Both of these groups survived through most of the Cretaceous period and may have become extinct at the same time as the dinosaurs, other marine reptiles, and much of the life on Earth 65 million years ago.

The early fossil record for marine turtles is relatively incomplete, and we don't know much about the earliest species. Turtles probably returned to freshwater environments and then on to the sea during the latter part of the Jurassic period. They generally remained small and probably stayed close to shore, and relative safety, for much of the Jurassic. During the Cretaceous, however, marine turtles became more diverse and much larger. Both the solid shell (like modern loggerhead turtles) and the leatherback varieties are represented as fossils. Possibly because their shells were much lighter and required fewer resources in their growth, some of these primitive leatherback turtles grew very large during the Late Cretaceous and literally became the size and weight of small automobiles. While the isolated fossil bones of these turtles had been found in other places, the first reasonably complete skeleton of a giant marine turtle was found in the Late Cretaceous rocks of western Kansas in 1871 by Edward Drinker "E. D." Cope. He gave it the name PROTOSTEGA GIGAS ▶, possibly because the construction of the shell reminded him of the rafters supporting the roof of a building. Although Cope somewhat exaggerated the length of the specimen he found, these turtles did grow to lengths (from the nose to the tip of the tail) of over 10 feet (3 meters). A closely related species, *Archelon ischyros*, which occurred later in the Cretaceous, was even larger, up to 15 feet in total length. The massive shells of these animals were as much as 7 to 8 feet across. The largest known leatherback turtles of today are about 6 feet in total length and weigh about 1100 pounds. *Protostega* and *Archelon* must have weighed in at several thousand pounds each. This extreme weight may have been the major factor in keeping them from growing even larger because the females of these species still had to come ashore periodically to lay their eggs. Crawling ponderously across the beach at high tide, scooping out a hole in the sand, laying eggs, and then returning to the sea before the sun rose and baked the turtle inside its shell would have been a difficult task for these large creatures. One specimen in the collection of the Sternberg Museum, located in Hays, Kansas, shows

KRONOSAURUS QUEENSLANDICUS
Order: Plesiosauria
Cretaceous Period • Australia
33 feet

WEBLINK
Discover more about giant turtles at the official Sea Monsters website.

LEFT: *These intimidating teeth belonged to a plesiosaur whose remains were discovered by miners in Australia in 1983.*

MOSASAUR

In 1967, teachers on a field trip in Kansas unearthed these mosasaur remains, a nearly complete 17-foot-long Platecarpus.

abrasions on the bones of the lower shell (plastron) that could have been caused as the turtle dragged its heavy body across the sand. Hatchling turtles were certainly easy prey for all kinds of marine predators, including a recent discovery in Australia that indicated baby turtles were fed upon by Early Cretaceous ichthyosaurs.

In Kansas, Late Cretaceous turtle remains are fairly common in the Smoky Hill chalk, but most of them are fragmentary specimens, which suggest that they are the remains of a predator's meal. The smaller varieties were certainly preyed upon by sharks and probably even by mosasaurs. In spite of their size, or maybe because of it, *Protostega* and *Archelon* became extinct at the end of the Cretaceous. However, even though they continue to be on the menu of many larger predators, the reproductive strategy of turtles (laying many eggs) allowed some smaller species to survive the extinction that eliminated the other great marine reptiles of the day.

Although they were the last of the sea monsters to evolve and return to the oceans of the Mesozoic, mosasaurs (whose name means "Meuse River lizard"—they were named for the river near their first discovery) were actually the first to be discovered and recognized as extinct marine creatures. The first partial skull and other remains were collected from Late Cretaceous limestone in The Netherlands about 1766.

Some of these specimens were placed in the Teylers Museum in Haarlem where they are still on exhibit today. These initial finds, however, did not draw the same scientific attention as the discovery made between 1770 and 1774 inside a limestone mine near Maastricht. There, workers cutting limestone blocks for building stones found a nearly complete skull of a large animal. In 1829, the creature was given a scientific name—*Mosasaurus hoffmanni*—in honor of the doctor who called it to the attention of the scientists of the day. The same skull is currently on exhibit in the National Museum of Natural History in Paris, France.

In the United States, several members of the Lewis and Clark expedition reported seeing the backbone of a 45-foot-long "fish" on a bluff of the Pierre shale above the Missouri River in South Dakota in October 1804. Unfortunately, the samples of this specimen that were sent back to Washington were lost, and we don't know for certain what the animal was. However, there are no fish of this size known from the Late Cretaceous, and although it might have been the rare skeleton of a long-necked plesiosaur, it is far more likely that it was the remains of a large mosasaur. The skull and partial skeleton of another mosasaur was discovered in South Dakota about 1830. Part of the skull was described and mistakenly named *Ichthyosaurus*

PLATE TECTONICS

ABOVE: *Geologic forces still work today as they did millions of years ago. Active underwater volcanoes create hydrothermal vents, like this one in the waters near French Polynesia.*

THE LANDMASSES OF THE EARTH are always on the move. The planet's uppermost layer (about 31 to 62 miles thick) is made of plates that slide over an underlying layer of molten rock. As these plates move, they bump into each other, resulting in massive collisions that shape the planet's lands and oceans. The continental formations of present-day Earth have been shaped over millions and millions of years. Earth-forms, as well as life-forms, keep evolving over time.

Two hundred million years ago, the landmass of Earth made up one supercontinent, called Pangaea. By that time, some of Earth's oldest mountains had been formed, like the northern Appalachians of the United States and the Caledonian Mountains in Scotland. The Tethys Ocean, geologic ancestor to the Mediterranean, was practically surrounded by land. Much of the globe was covered by water, the Panthalassic Ocean.

Over time, Eurasia moved apart from the conglomerate, slowly dividing into Antarctica, South America, and North America. One hundred million years ago, rifts in the continental landmasses were developing into the oceans we're familiar with today. A great shallow body of water nearly bisected North America: It was the Western Interior Sea, home to many of the Earth's most successful species of marine reptile.

200 Million Years Ago:

When the first dinosaurs roamed the planet, most of the landmasses of the Earth were joined in a worldwide continent that stretched nearly pole to pole.

100 Million Years Ago:

When sea monsters dominated the waters, great rifts in the world-continent had deepened into oceans, and waterways covered more than 80 percent of the globe.

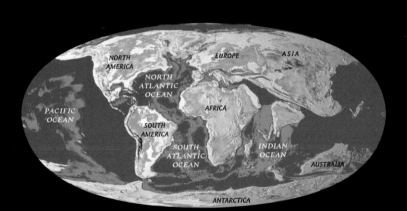

50 Million Years Ago:

Today's highest mountains, including the Alps and the Himalayas, were formed only after the end of the Cretaceous period, 65 million years ago, when the mass extinction of the monstrous marine reptiles and dinosaurs occurred.

Present Day:

Some continental shapes on the globe today are relatively new in formation: the Isthmus of Panama and Australia. Scientists believe that plate interactions in East Africa may eventually cause the Horn of Africa to break away from the rest of the continent.

missouriensis, but the rest of the specimen was later taken to Germany where it was prepared, recognized to be that of a mosasaur, and called *Mosasaurus missouriensis*. Because of its three-dimensional preservation, the skull of this mosasaur specimen was even more informative than the remains of *Mosasaurus hoffmanni*.

There were many kinds of mosasaurs living during the Late Cretaceous. Mosasaurs like *Hainosaurus* grew to lengths of more than 50 feet and evolved into a variety of shapes, sizes, and ecological adaptations, including species (like *Globidens*) that were specialized in eating hard-shelled prey such as clams. Others were much smaller and well adapted to feed on smaller animals close to shore. These adaptations allowed mosasaurs as a group to take over the oceans of the Earth and become the dominant marine predator for millions of years just before the end of the Cretaceous. Their bones have been discovered from Alaska to the islands off the coast of Antarctica and on every continent in between. Thousands of specimens have been collected just from ◄ KANSAS alone, and their remains are relatively abundant in many Late Cretaceous marine rocks from around the world.

The oceans of the Earth during the 180 million years or so of the Mesozoic era were certainly very dangerous places. Giant ichthyosaurs and pliosaurs would have made the Jurassic and Early Cretaceous seas a risky place for anything smaller than them. The arrival of mosasaurs during the Late Cretaceous increased the risk dramatically because of their size, numbers and ability to go after even larger prey. Given that they were abundant in the shallow seas that covered and surrounded the continents of the time, it can be said that the oceans of the Late Cretaceous were probably the most dangerous seas ever on this planet.

WEBLINK

Discover more about the fossil finds of Kansas at the official Sea Monsters website.

THE EVOLUTION OF SEA MONSTERS

Life on Earth evolved first in the sea where the early environment was more favorable than on the barren land. Many of the earliest life forms either were able to capture the energy they needed from the sun (photosynthetic), from the chemistry of the water in which they lived in (chemosynthetic), or from feeding on the organic detritus that accumulated on the sea floor. As marine life became larger and more complex, an arms race began when some forms developed mouth parts, including teeth and jaws, to feed on other animals, and these other forms developed armor to resist those teeth and jaws. Giant scorpion-like invertebrates, huge armored fish, and early sharks preyed on other life-forms in the sea around them.

As life began to colonize the land, the arms race continued on both fronts. Land animals, however, began to evolve into more efficient, better armed, and more diverse

This mosasaur lived about 85 million years ago and had a set of teeth on the roof of its mouth (visible here beneath its eye socket) to grasp its prey.

forms, including the giant-sized dinosaurs that we are familiar with today. Competition for food and other resources was fierce among the many kinds of terrestrial animals. The oceans offered a rich source of food, and little competition, to those terrestrial animals that could adapt to living in it. Some of the reptiles living along the shore took advantage of the availability of these food resources and essentially lived in both worlds, feeding in the ocean but returning to the land to rest and breed. Eventually some of those animals became so well adapted to life in the ocean that they cut their ties to the land and returned completely to a marine existence.

There were some "experiments" among land dwelling reptiles during Permian time, and many more during the Early Triassic period, but ichthyosaurs appear to be the first terrestrial reptile group to successfully reenter and dominate the oceans. Apparently there was little competition and no other major predators of the time that were able to resist their rapid expansion into the Triassic seas. Within the space of a few million years, they had evolved into many diverse forms and grown to gigantic sizes. Some remains found recently in Canada suggest an ichthyosaur that was nearly as large as a blue whale, the largest living thing in our modern world. Mostly the ichthyosaurs fed on invertebrates (cephalopods) and small fish. They were able to rule the seas for millions of years. Ichthyosaurs appeared to reach their greatest diversity during the Late Triassic and Early Jurassic periods. Their numbers and species dwindled rapidly

Two fierce mosasaurs circle each other warily as they prepare to do battle. These beasts probably competed with each other for territory and fought off any interlopers.

ALBUM: A MODERN MONSTER?

The plesiosaur called Thalassomedon had a 20-foot-long neck, half its body length. This shape may have allowed it to hunt with stealth, reaching prey while its body remained unseen in the murky depths below.

FANTASTIC, TERRIFYING SEA MONSTERS appear in stories told all over the world. In the Bible, the sea creature Leviathan is described as the "coiling serpent . . . the monster of the sea" (Isaiah 27:1). Lakota Sioux legends recount how the Unktehila, the "evil water monsters," were destroyed by the Wakinyan, the Thunder Beings. In Greek myth, Perseus saves the beautiful Andromeda from being devoured by a sea monster. For centuries, these creatures were murky beings of legend, but when mid-20th-century visitors to Scotland's Loch Ness produced photographs of a creature said to live in the lake, the images raised the question: If you could photograph the Loch Ness monster, must it be real, or is it only a modern legend?

Claims that a "horrible great beastie" lives in Loch Ness, a finger lake in north-central Scotland, date back to the 1870s. One observer in 1908, for instance, swore he saw a creature with an eel-like head and a long tail basking at the lake's surface. A new road opened in 1933, allowing easier access to the lake than ever before and sparking a flurry of new sightings. Always eager for a sensational story, the *Daily Mail* sent Marmaduke Wetherell, a colorful big-game hunter, up to Scotland to scout out the creature. Wetherell claimed to have found four-toed footprints of the monster on the shores of the lake.

PHOTOGRAPH OF LOCH MONSTER : EXCLUSIVE

21st 1934 Daily Mail

A mysterious carcass washed
ashore at Loch Ness.

Caught on videotape in 1983, unidentified splashes break the surface of Loch Ness.

The most famous shot of Nessie ever taken

An inaccurate vision of a sea monster encounter.

These fossilized vertebrae were found along the shores of Loch Ness. Experts feel they were planted there.

The most famous photograph of the legendary creature was taken in 1934 by a retired British surgeon named Robert Wilson. Wilson's image confirmed for the public imagination that the Loch Ness monster must have been shaped something like the long-necked elasmosaur, if such a creature could hold its head up above the water. His photograph became the iconic emblem of the Loch Ness monster that tourists all hoped they would see. Another photograph, taken in 1955 by Peter MacNab, a Scottish bank manager, rekindled belief in the legend for another generation, even though it seemed to show nothing more than something long and large moving in the water.

Skeptics wasted no time in attacking this new "evidence." Investigators proved that Wetherell's discovered footprints were actually created by Wetherell himself; he had made the tracks with a stuffed hippo's foot. MacNab's photo was debunked as a doctored negative early on, but Wilson's iconic image remained popular for decades. In 1984 an article in the British Journal of Photography argued that, given other details, the object in Wilson's photograph could not be more than three feet long. Perhaps, the author suggested, it was an otter or a floating bird. If the object were a modern-day elasmosaur, the position of the neck and head shown in the photo would be physically impossible.

The mighty Thalassomedon *slashed sideways at prey, trapping it inside interlocking teeth. Crocodiles use a similar hunting technique today.*

in the Late Jurassic, culminating in an apparent extinction event near the Jurassic-Cretaceous boundary. At the beginning of the Early Cretaceous, there were probably only one or two species left, and by the beginning of the Late Cretaceous, roughly 100 million years ago, even they had become extinct for reasons not yet fully understood. It may have increased competition from larger fish for the same prey, or their primary prey (cephalopods), into faster, more elusive species that been due to plesiosaurs and a major die-off of or simply that fish had evolved were harder to catch.

About the same time as ichthyosaurs were conquering the oceans of Earth, small, shore-dwelling lizards called nothosaurs were beginning to evolve into larger, better-adapted forms that spent more and more time in the sea. Eventually, their limbs became nearly solid paddles which enabled them to fly through the water like four-winged penguins. At some point in the Late Triassic, the first plesiosaurs also left the land behind and began to live their entire lives at sea. As they became larger and more diverse, they probably competed for the same food resources that the ichthyosaurs were feeding upon. Preserved stomach contents show us that they ate mostly cephalopods during Jurassic time and were switching from these soft-bodied invertebrates to a predominately fish diet during the Late Cretaceous. Plesiosaurs went through several extinction events between the Jurassic and Cretaceous, but they seemed to always manage to rebound. During the Late Cretaceous, direct competition with or predation by mosasaurs may have forced plesiosaurs into lesser roles as predators. Their remains are found around the world from near the end of the Cretaceous, but they are not nearly as numerous as those of mosasaurs.

Turtles apparently were conservative enough and fed low enough on the food chain that they did not have to compete with other marine reptiles for food or other resources. They also maintained a connection with the land, retaining their ability to move across sand beaches in order to come back periodically and lay their eggs. In the process, they were able to become large and relatively numerous during the Late

HENODUS CHELYOPS

Order: *Placodontia*

Triassic Period • Europe

9 feet

Cretaceous. They were sea monsters in size, but relatively benign ones compared to the other predatory varieties.

Like the plesiosaurs, the mosasaurs also evolved from near-shore dwelling lizards. In the case of mosasaurs, their time was the earliest part of the Late Cretaceous, and we believe their ancestors were small (4 to 6 feet) lizards called aigialosaurs. These ancestral mosasauroids have been found in many places around the world, and it appears likely that different kinds of early mosasaurs may have entered the ocean in several places about the same time. Like the ichthyosaurs and plesiosaurs, once the MOSASAURS ▶ entered the ocean they evolved, rapidly diversified, and grew much larger. In part, this may have been the result of having little or no competition for the role as top predator. By then ichthyosaurs were extinct; the last of the big-headed plesiosaurs (pliosaurs) were also on their way out. There were, however, large prehistoric sharks that we know made life difficult for mosasaurs for a few million years, and they certainly had to compete with large predatory fish, but they were able to reproduce, grow fast enough, and compete for food resources in ways that

Paleontologist George R. Wieland stands alongside an 11-foot-tall Archelon ischyros, *an ancient marine turtle discovered in South Dakota in 1895.*

WEBLINK

Discover more about mosasaurs at the official Sea Monsters website.

overcame the competition. They appear to have been very aggressive and capable predators. Within a relatively short time, geologically speaking, they were the largest carnivore and undisputed top predator in all of the oceans of the Earth. It appears that a collapse of the marine ecosystem about 65 million years ago led to their downfall. In this case, however, their extinction was a good thing for humans. Sharing the oceans of today with anything like a giant mosasaur is a terrifying proposition.

The mosasaurs, and possibly a few plesiosaurs, were the last of the great marine reptiles, and the last of the Mesozoic-era sea monsters. At the end of the Age of Dinosaurs, the oceans were hard hit and many species became extinct. Life in the seas rebounded quickly and new kinds of marine creatures vied for the title of sea monster. After the Cretaceous, mammals replaced the reptiles as the ruling class of animals on the land, and within a few million years, some mammals followed the earlier path of the marine reptiles and also returned to the sea. One of the early whales (*Basilosaurus*, misnamed as "king of the lizards") looked very much like a mosasaur and fed primarily on fish and squid. Mother Nature didn't give up easily on the overall successful mosasaur design, although this early whale also swam by moving its tail up and down instead of side to side like a mosasaur.

Also deserving of the title of "sea monster" was a monstrously large shark called *Carcharodon megalodon*. Estimated to be as long as 50 feet and having blade-like, serrated teeth that were 6 to 7 inches tall, these giants probably fed on early sea mammals for a few million years before they, too, became extinct. The modern blue whale (100 feet long, 200 tons) is certainly one of the largest animals that has ever lived, but left alone, it is of little danger to anything but tiny krill, hardly good press for a real "sea monster." As large as these whales and sharks were, however, they were probably never as numerous as the great marine reptiles of the Mesozoic era and never achieved the worldwide dominance of the mosasaurs.

BACULITE

Order: *Ammonitida*
Cretaceous Period • Worldwide
4 feet

RIGHT: *A lone* Dolichorhynchops *scans its shallow surroundings. Paleontologists believe these creatures frequented coastal waters when food was plentiful.*

EARTH DURING THE LATE CRETACEOUS

The planet Earth is in a continuous state of change. Our environment may not appear to change significantly during our lifetimes, or even in the time since our grandparents and great-grandparents were born, but Earth and its climate is changing slowly. The bodies of land that we call continents and assume to be

immovable masses of rock continue to move slowly apart, floating on the molten liquid core of the planet, driven by forces that are not completely understood. The geological forces that cause earthquakes and volcanoes, and those that erode the land, are continually modifying the surface of the Earth. Justifiable concerns have arisen over the recent rapidity by which global warming appears to be occurring and the influence of humans in the generation of greenhouse gases. But on a larger timescale, Earth is still recovering from the last Ice Age more than 10,000 years ago. A look even deeper into the Earth's geologic past indicates that, on the average, temperatures have been somewhat warmer than what is considered "normal" today. Much of human history and prehistory has occurred during times which were cooler than the overall average temperature of the Earth over the last several hundred million years. The Earth has generally been warmer than today, and the Cretaceous period is a typical example of such a warmer time.

During the Late Cretaceous, the Earth was several degrees warmer than today. There were no ice caps at the north and south poles. Trees and dinosaurs lived as far north and south as there was land. Because water was not locked up in ice caps and glaciers, sea levels were much higher and it is likely that as much as 85 percent of the Earth's surface was covered by oceans (as compared to about 71 percent today). It was truly a water planet. Many of these seas were relatively shallow and covered the low-lying areas of today's modern continents. Almost the entire midwest of North America was inundated by what is called the Western Interior Sea. This shallow sea and others like it around the world were very productive and provided abundant sources of food for larger predators such as large sharks, bony fish, and giant marine reptiles.

During the Mesozoic era, life on the land was dominated by large herds of plant-eating dinosaurs and a much smaller number of medium to large carnivorous dinosaurs. There were the usual assortment of smaller animals, including birds and mammals, but none monopolized the landscape as much as the dinosaurs did. Looking very similar to what we see today, large forests of both coniferous and deciduous trees flourished. Long grasses were just evolving, and the complex relationship that developed between flowering plants and pollinating insects (like bees) was well under way. Aside from the strange-looking dinosaurs, the terrestrial environment would not have looked greatly different from what we see around the world today.

In many respects, however, life in the ocean took a different direction. The base of the Late Cretaceous marine food chain, as well as the modern one, depends upon

BLUE WHALE

Order: *Cetacea*

Paleogene Period • Worldwide

110 feet

microscopic algae and other photosynthetic organisms (called producers) to convert sunlight into the complex organic molecules used for growth and reproduction. They in turn were fed upon by larger organisms called consumers. During the Late Cretaceous, most of the primary consumers in the ocean depended on the productivity of these single-cell organisms. In fact, just about every creature above the level of the single-celled photosynthetic producers was a consumer. Some, like larger microorganisms and the tiny larvae of fish, cephalopods, and other marine life, fed on these microscopic plants. Unlike the land, as far as we can tell from the fossil record, there were no large herbivores that grazed on sea grasses or large filter-feeding marine animals comparable to modern basking sharks or baleen whales during the Late Cretaceous.

Almost everything, from the billions and billions of fish the size of your little finger, to giant mosasaurs, was carnivorous and came equipped with jaws and teeth and an appetite honed specifically for that purpose. Some of the smallest fish (like *Enchodus*) found preserved as fossils from that time came equipped with oversized teeth that are large enough to earn them the nickname of "saber-toothed salmon." These, in turn, were fed upon by larger fish, including their larger cousins, which were then preyed upon by even larger fish, sharks, and mosasaurs. One of the largest bony fish ever known, *Xiphactinus audax*, grew to a maximum length of about 18 feet and was capable of swallowing a fish up to half its length (sometimes with fatal results).

Earth was warmer than it is today when dinosaurs, like this Tyrannosaurus rex, *lived. Nearly 85 pecent of the world was covered by water.*

Two short-necked plesio-
saurs, *both* Dolichorhynchops, *dive and plunge
through a large school of*
Caproberyx *fish.*

There were sharks, like *Cretoxyrhina mantelli*, that grew as large as modern great whites. Smaller sharks, like the *Squalicorax,* or crow shark, fed on fish and scavenged carcasses. Elasmosaurs and polycotylids of the Late Cretaceous mostly fed on fish and the abundant squid and other cephalopods, and were not a threat to anything larger than their small prey. Turtles probably ate about the same thing as they do today— jellyfish, sea grasses, small crustaceans, and occasionally even scavenged carcasses. Pteranodons and marine birds fed mostly on small fish. At the very top of this "eat and be eaten" pyramid were the mosasaurs. These medium- to giant-sized predators apparently ate anything they could swallow whole, like fish, squid, and possibly ammonites, which were abundantly available. Occasionally larger mosasaurs, such as *Tylosaurus,* could devour other kinds of prey such as sharks, marine birds, smaller mosasaurs, and even an occasional short-necked plesiosaur, like a *Dolichorhynchops.*

Longer than 30 feet, heavier than 11 tons, teeth the size of bananas: Kronosaurus *was one of Earth's most powerful predators 100 million years ago.*

Often called "The Age of the Dinosaurs," the Mesozoic era spanned 185 million years. Geologists have divided it into three distinct periods:

MESOZOIC ERA = *251.0–65.5 M.Y.A.*

TRIASSIC PERIOD = *251.0–199.6 M.Y.A.*

JURASSIC PERIOD = *199.6–145.5 M.Y.A.*

CRETACEOUS PERIOD = *145.5–65.5 M.Y.A.*

The preservation of so many large predators in the fossil record is a good indication of just how productive the marine ecosystem was during the Late Cretaceous. In comparison, relatively few small fish and other animals have been collected. In part that is because most of them were consumed by predators or eaten by scavengers shortly after death. We know that there had to be many smaller species in huge numbers to support the dietary needs of the many large carnivores.

In light of all we have come to know through careful excavation and analysis of geologic and fossil remains, a picture begins to come into view of a watery world from millions of years ago. Suddenly the imaginary shapes in the corners of antique maps take on a different dimension. Sea monsters did once roam the oceans of this planet, and fossil finders and paleontologists keep turning up finds to tell us more about the sea monsters and their world.

GLASSES ON

Soaring gracefully above
the waters of the
Western Interior Sea
is a Pteranodon. *These*
flying reptiles dined
on fish but had no teeth.

LIFE ON EARTH DURING THE LATE CRETACEOUS PERIOD looked quite different than it does today. Large reptilian predators flew in the air, walked on the land, and swam in the seas. Tyranosaurids, above, like the *Gorgosaurus*, roamed the land in search of prey. They were fearsome hunters, but also not above scavenging their meals. Below the surface of the Western Interior Sea, the water teemed with different forms of life. Large schools of *Enchodus* fish were an abundant food source for larger fish, like the *Xiphactinus*, and for marine reptiles, like the four-flippered *Dolichorhynchops*, opposite above and below. Some believe that these schools of *Enchodus* would migrate annually from the shallows to the deeper, open waters, forcng the predators who dined on them make the journey as well. In the deeper water, danger often lurked.

Tylosaurs lived at the top of
the food chain during the
Late Cretaceous period. These
fearsome predators could
grow up to 40 feet long.

GLASSES OFF
FOR NEXT PAGE

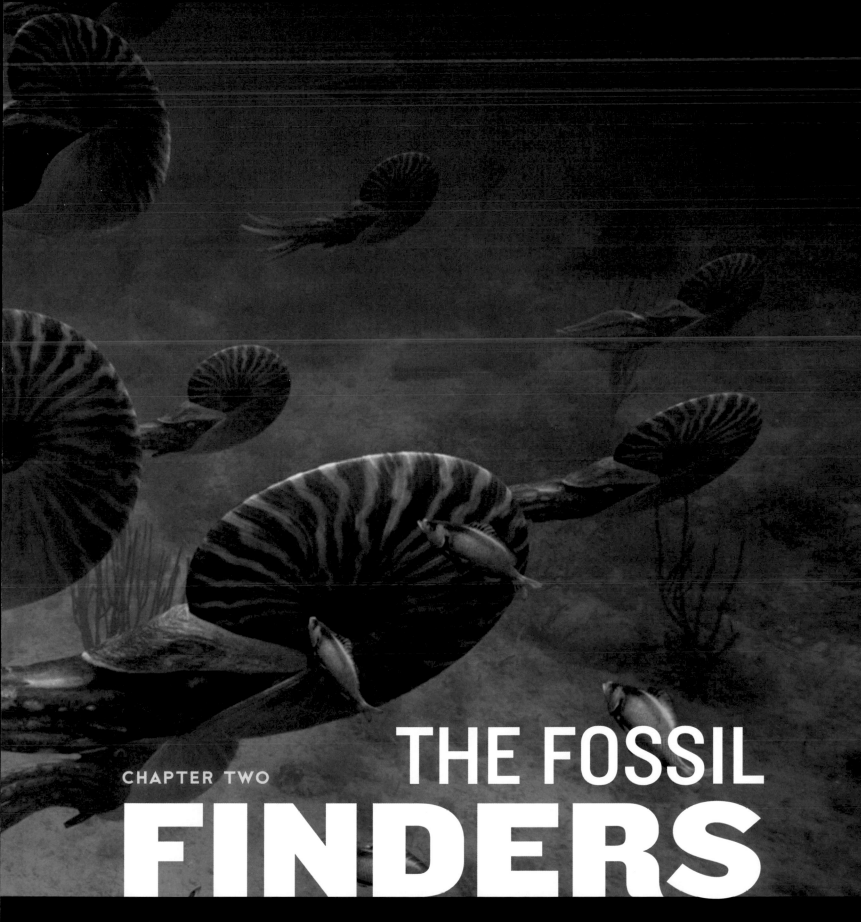

CHAPTER TWO

THE FOSSIL FINDERS

A group of ammonites drifts along the sea floor. Ammonite fossils often help paleontologists identify geologic time periods.

XIPHACTINUS AUDAX
Order: *Ichthyodectiformes*
Cretaceous Period • North America
20 feet

T WAS SPRING IN WESTERN KANSAS, 1867, AND DR. THEOPHILUS H. Turner—the military surgeon posted at Fort Wallace, the most westerly in Kansas of the few U.S. Army outposts scattered along the route of the Union Pacific Railroad between Kansas City and Denver—was exploring the exposures of Pierre shale near the fort. He often spent his off-duty hours hunting buffalo and antelope or collecting mineral specimens. In the brief time he had been in Kansas, he had learned a lot about the western prairie. But that day he came upon something neither he, nor anyone else, had ever seen. Poking about in an eroded exposure of dark gray shale, he noticed a connected series of large black objects. They were neither rocks nor clods of dirt. To Dr. Turner's educated eye, they looked like the bones of a large animal buried in the rock. As he dug away at the loose pieces of shale, he began to realize that he had come upon the backbone of some extinct monster, buried under the western Kansas plains.

LEFT: *Searching for their next meal, fierce* Xiphactinus *fish are on the prowl. These giant predators could grow up to 17 feet long and eat fish as large as 6 feet.*

MAJOR FOSSIL DISCOVERIES

Fossil finds from the last 200 years have revealed much about sea monsters.

1770

1780

WHO: Dr. J. L. Hoffmann
WHEN: ca 1780
WHERE: The Meuse River Maastricht, the Netherlands
WHAT: Recognized the importance of the first known mosasaur skull, which was eventually named *Mosasaurus hoffmanni* in his honor

1790

1800

1810

WHO: Mary Anning
WHEN: ca 1820–1821
WHERE: Lyme Regis, England
WHAT: Discovered the first nearly complete plesiosaur skeleton

1820

1830

1840

WHO: Dr. Theophilus H. Turner
WHEN: 1867
WHERE: Fort Wallace, Kansas
WHAT: Discovered one of the largest elasmosaurs ever found, the *Elasmosaurus platyurus* assembled by E. D. Cope

1850

1860

1870

1880

Even a modern reproduction evokes wonder at the discovery of an

entire Gillicus *fish trapped in the rib cage of its more monstrous predator.*

1890

WHO: Charles & George Sternberg
WHEN: 1900
WHERE: Logan County, Kansas
WHAT: Found a new plesiosaur species, *Dolichorhynchops osborni*

1900

1910

WHO: Charles H. Sternberg
WHEN: 1918
WHERE: Logan County, Kansas
WHAT: A nearly complete *Tylosaurus* skeleton with the digested bones of a juvenile plesiosaur inside, the first evidence that mosasaurs ate plesiosaurs

1920

1930

1940

1950

WHO: George Sternberg
WHEN: 1952
WHERE: Gove County, Kansas
WHAT: A specimen of *Xiphactinus* fish with its well-preserved last meal, a *Gillicus* fish, inside

1960

1970

1980

WHO: Elizabeth Nicholls
WHEN: 1999–2001
WHERE: British Columbia, CAN
WHAT: The largest ichthyosaur ever discovered: *Shonisaurus sikanniensis,* which measured over 70 feet long

1990

2000

2010

Huge chalk formations in Kansas, such as Monument Rock, have provided a scenic background for fossil hunters since the mid-1800s.

Turner dug out a few of the vertebrae that day and later he gave three of them to a railroad surveyor to carry back to Philadelphia. Each was several inches long, heavy and roughly spool-shaped. Several months later, the railroad surveyor delivered the vertebrae to E. D. Cope, then a 28-year-old naturalist and paleontologist at Philadelphia's Academy of Natural Sciences. Educated as a herpetologist, Cope immediately recognized the importance of the bones and had a hunch that they may be the remains of a large marine reptile, called a plesiosaur, from a prehistoric era that paleontologists in Europe and the U.S. were just beginning to comprehend.

Encouraged by Cope's response, Dr. Turner returned to the site the following winter, this time prepared for an all-out excavation. Some time around Christmas of 1867, he and other soldiers from Fort Wallace dug into the Kansas shale, using picks and shovels to extract the massive array of bones that Turner had discovered. Turner wrote in a letter to his brother and reported that he had collected "something over thirty-five feet" of the monster's vertebrae, and "a large amount of bony matter contained in a very hard stony matrix."

All told, Turner and the others excavated some 900 pounds of bones and supporting material. It was the largest fossil collected anywhere in the world up until that time, and the beginning of a gold rush of fossil finding in the western Kansas plains. Turner's discovery traveled by military wagon train, then by rail, to Cope in Philadelphia, who announced in March of 1868 that Dr. Turner had discovered a new and heretofore unknown kind of plesiosaur, which he called *Elasmosaurus platyurus*, in the Kansas shale. The hunt was on, and Turner's plesiosaur was the first of many fossil discoveries proving that sea monsters once reigned in the oceans of Kansas.

HOW FOSSILS FORM

Despite the considerable importance of Dr. Turner's discovery, the first of many in Kansas, fossils of sea monsters are relatively rare. Of the few specimens we have in museums, most are fragmentary. All of the remains ever found represent a tiny fraction of the hundreds of thousands of these animals that must have lived over many millions of years on Earth. Many sea monsters lived, but few left valuable fossils behind. Becoming a fossil involves a series of unlikely events occurring at the right time and place and in the correct order in order to preserve the bones so that a fossil finder, millions of years later, has something to excavate and study.

When an animal dies, many natural processes go to work. In most cases, predators, scavengers, and decomposers consume the remains relatively quickly. The biological materials contained in a dead animal are valuable to the ecosystem, and very little goes to waste. Recently it has been shown that even the remains of giant blue whales that sink to the bottom of the deep ocean are totally consumed within a few short years by fish, invertebrates, bacteria, and other organisms. For remains to become fossilized, all those natural processes have to be minimized or prevented altogether. Marine environments encourage fossilization because sand, mud, or limey sediments may cover the remains of a dead animal before other animals consume it.

Various parts and pieces of an animal's remains sometimes escape being digested as food and fall to the sea bottom, where they may also be preserved as fossils. In other cases, an animal might bloat and float as it decomposes, slowly falling apart as it drifts across the water, its limbs, skull, and vertebrae sinking separately to the sea bottom.

This fossil is the first articulated plesiosaur ever found. Pioneering fossil finder Mary Anning discovered it in Lyme Regis, Dorset, England, in the early 19th century.

After a long life, the Dolichorhynchops dies in the shallows and sinks to the bottom where her remains will be preserved, and, over millions of years, fossilized.

In the film Sea Monsters, *a* Dolichorhynchops *fossil is excavated from a riverbank. The actress here re-creates the careful work that paleontologists must do to extricate remains.*

Once remains land on the soft, muddy bottom, invertebrates and smaller organisms, such as bacteria, slowly continue the process of decomposing the flesh surrounding the bones. Occasionally, the mud on the sea bottom seals off portions of a carcass, so that interesting things like soft tissue or cartilage, skin impressions, or even a last meal are preserved along with the bones.

In a matter of a few days or weeks, the bones have been completely defleshed. When fine, chalky sediments build up over them, decomposition of the living matter continues, thanks to invertebrates and microorganisms small enough to do their work without disturbing the bones. Under similar circumstances—such as those in Kansas's Smoky Hill Chalk, where conditions are favorable to preservation—entire skeletons can be well preserved.

The remains of the buried animal undergo a slow process of fossilization as sediment continues to accumulate over it. The limey mud around the bones is squeezed and compacted by the pressure of the overlying sediments, forcing most of the water out and leaving a fine-grained matrix composed mostly of billions of tiny calcite scales from marine plankton. Eventually the dewatered mud hardens into chalk, entombing what is left of the sea monster and other animals. There, encased in that chalky matrix, the fossilized bones of prehistoric animals remain hidden, preserved for millions of years until geological events bring them back to the surface and those bones are again exposed.

In Kansas—and, in fact, in most of the North American midwest—the waters of the Interior Sea receded near the end of the Cretaceous period, around 65 million years ago. The same massive geological processes that raised the mountain chains in western North America lifted rocks that had been buried at the bottom of the sea to above sea level. Once exposed to weathering, these relatively soft sedimentary rocks began to erode away. Streams and rivers slowly cut channels through the layers of shale, chalk, limestone, and sandstone. Over the past 60 million years, they carried away a large portion of the sediments that once formed the seafloor. These eroded sediments washed down the tributaries of the Mississippi River and were again deposited underwater as a part of its huge mud

delta spreading out into the Gulf of Mexico. As this was happening, thousands of fossils eroded out as well. Fossil remains of sea monsters, fish, pterasaurs, prehistoric birds, and even dinosaurs were broken down, weathered away, and washed downstream. Only a small portion of the original fossil record now remains in the geologic formation that we call the Smoky Hill Chalk, still buried under the surface of Kansas, Colorado, Nebraska, and South Dakota.

A discovery like the one made by Dr. Turner in 1867 is a lucky one. Fossil remains just happened to become exposed at the surface at about the same time that human investigators became scientifically interested in finding fossils. A few vertebrae, the edge of the skull, or the bones of a paddle become visible along the side of a hill, and the long process of digging, collecting, and reconstructing a sea monster can begin.

THE FIRST DISCOVERIES

Although fossils have been eroding out of rocks for as long as man has been around, the first recorded discovery of what we call sea monsters did not occur until between 1770 and 1774, when the massive skull of a mosasaur was collected from a limestone mine near the Meuse River in The Netherlands. Similar bones and partial skeletons had been collected as curiosities for many years, interpreted as the remains of large fish, whales, or crocodiles. In this case, however, Dr. J. L. Hoffman, a military surgeon, learned of the discovery and shared it with prominent scientists of the time, including the French anatomist Baron Georges Cuvier. It was Cuvier who determined that the remains came from an animal unlike any alive on Earth at the time, and first proposed the concept of extinction. After years of study, it was determined to be the skull of an

The camera captures a distant view of Monument Rocks in Kansas. The chalk layers are clearly visible, even from far away.

extinct marine animal, closely related to monitor lizards such as Komodo dragons. The creature was eventually called *Mosasaurus* (meaning "Meuse River lizard"), its species name *hoffmanni,* in honor of the man who recognized the scientific importance of the specimen.

In the 1820s, a young Englishwoman named Mary Anning became an important contributor to the knowledge of sea monsters. She lived near Lyme Regis, on the southern coast of England, and often collected shells, including ammonite fossils, to sell as curios. She began to notice fossilized bones in among the shells along the shore and ultimately became famous in the scientific circles of the day for her ability to locate and collect the bones of these strange creatures. Anning was the first person to discover fossil remains from the sea monsters that we now identify as ichthyosaurs and plesiosaurs. Additional specimens were found about the same time in limestone quarries in Europe, where workers would see the bones as they cut out blocks for building or dug clay for bricks. It is worth noting here

that fossils from three major groups of marine reptiles—ichthyosaurs, plesiosaurs, and mosasaurs—had already been discovered before the term "Dinosauria" was coined by Sir Richard Owen in 1842. These early discoveries of sea monster remains contributed tremendously to our early understanding of the modern concepts of extinction and evolution.

In the United States, fragmentary remains of marine reptiles had been collected along the East Coast, primarily in New Jersey. A few vertebrae and fragments of jaws with teeth were recognized as coming from the same kinds of marine reptiles found in Europe. In September 1804, four members of the Lewis and Clark expedition wrote in their journals about finding the "backbone of a 45-foot fish" exposed on a bluff overlooking the Missouri River farther west in today's South Dakota. They sent some of the vertebrae back to Washington, but the samples never arrived. Additional mosasaur remains were found in New Jersey's greensands, a deposit of marine sediments, around 1818. Fur trappers and gentleman explorers continued to find similar fossil remains in the West, and slowly but surely evidence of sea monsters in

The first recorded discovery of sea monster remains occurred in The Netherlands in the early 1700s, more than a century before Darwin articulated the theory of evolution.

C OLLECTION, PRESERVATION, AND PROTECTION of fossils were the biggest challenges encountered by early paleontologists in the 1860s and 1870s. Although well preserved in the Smoky Hill chalk of Kansas, the ancient bones were often extremely fragile once removed from the ground. Early paleontologists experimented with ways to remove them, pack them, ship them back East, and reconstruct them with the full information of how they lay in relation to one another, but these methods proved imperfect and often important data could be lost in the transition.

The Sternbergs devised a method that would revolutionize fossil collection and preservation. In an 1884 article, "Directions for Collecting Vertebrate Fossils," Charles Sternberg suggested plaster as a way to avoid these problems and a means of recovering specimens more safely and completely from the field. In the years to come, Sternberg perfected this important fieldwork collection technique. Eventually he was able to use the method to recover large fossils in their entirety. The technique continues to be used in the field today and has even been modified for specimens requiring closer examination and possibly repair. These can be collected in "jackets" of plaster and burlap that can later be removed from the find for closer examination.

Friends and neighbors often drove out into the chalk beds of Logan County, Kansas, to watch the Sternbergs as they collected fossils.

◄ STEP ONE:

In 1952, George Sternberg recovered a remarkable 13-foot *Xiphactinus* fossil from the Kansas chalk. A nearly complete specimen, the large fish also contained the remains of its last meal, a 6-foot *Gillicus* fish, inside. The team first carefully excavated the rock and materials surrounding the find. Next they built a wooden frame around it to protect the fossil.

◄ STEP TWO:

Once the frame was in place, the team poured plaster over the fossil. As Charles Sternberg described the technique, a field collector would "cover the specimen with two or three inches of plaster of Paris and allow it to set." The hardened plaster, wrote Sternberg, "gives a fine protection to delicate bones."

◄ STEP THREE:

Next, after waiting for the plaster to harden, the team carefully dug underneath (also called "undercutting") the plaster-embedded specimen to free it from the underlying chalk. It was imperative to remove debris and soil from all sides of the specimen before trying to move it to make sure everything stayed intact.

◄ STEP FOUR:

To ease the excavation, Sternberg designed the wooden frame to be easily cut in two pieces, so each one could be hoisted out, one at a time. The team lined up and then turned the casted piece up and over. The bones, secure in their wooden frame and plaster coating, were safely excavated from the soil.

George F. Sternberg, second-generation fossil hunter, proudly poses with prize finds of 1928.

North America began to accumulate. A fur trapper working along the Missouri River in what is now South Dakota found the "skeleton of an alligator-animal" in a large limestone concretion. A small portion of those remains was mistakenly declared to be part of the skull of an ichthyosaur by a medical doctor in Philadelphia. Later, in the late 1830s a German nobleman, Prince Maximilian of Wied-Neuwied, traveled with the Swiss artist Karl Bodmer among Indians living in the wilds of today's Nebraska and South Dakota. Along the way, they acquired this specimen and shipped the bones back to Germany. There Dr. August Goldfuss prepared and described the fossils, which were properly identified as a mosasaur. Today, they are still on display today in the Goldfuss Museum, University of Bonn, Germany.

By the 1860s, American scientists had begun the serious study of paleontology. The discovery of the first skull of *Tylosaurus proriger* in western Kansas in 1868 brought two of the nation's most prominent paleontologists, E. D. Cope and Othniel Charles "O. C." Marsh, to the state—and the rush for fossils was on. While Cope represented Philadelphia's Academy of the Natural Sciences, his rival, Marsh, collected fossil specimens for the Yale College (now part of the collection at Yale University's Peabody Museum of Natural History). Marsh's scientific expeditions and the collectors hired by Cope recovered literally thousands of sea monster specimens from western Kansas during the next decade. Since that time, remains of similar prehistoric marine reptile species have been discovered on every continent, including the islands off the coast of Antarctica. New species are still being discovered, named, and described at a steady pace even today.

THE STERNBERG DYNASTY

In the late 1860s the Union Pacific Railroad was being constructed across the plains to connect Kansas City, Missouri, and Denver, Colorado. Western Kansas was the unsettled frontier, and the U.S. Army established forts across the state to protect the railroad workers and others from Indian attacks: Fort Riley, Fort Harker, Fort Hays, and, farthest west, Fort Wallace. Assigned to each garrison were one or more doctors, arguably among the most educated men in the state and often interested in many aspects of science besides medicine.

In 1866, DR. GEORGE STERNBERG ▶ brought his avid interest in geology and paleontology to his assignment at Fort Harker in central Kansas. When he first moved to Kansas, he began collecting fossil leaf imprints from the nearby Dakota sandstone. When he was sent even farther west during the campaigns against the Indians, Sternberg continued collecting fossils and bones, including a 16-inch-long piece of the front fin of a prehistoric fish called *Xiphactinus*. Many of the specimens collected by George M. Sternberg are in the Smithsonian Institution's collection today, still inscribed with his signature. Sternberg went on to become surgeon-general of the U.S. Army during the Spanish-American War and is better recognized for his contributions to medicine and bacteriology than for his discoveries in paleontology.

After acquiring a ranch south of Fort Harker in the late 1860s, Sternberg arranged for his parents and siblings to move to Kansas. His younger brother, Charles H. Sternberg, was equally fascinated by the fossils that he found in the surrounding hills. He was 17 years old when he moved to western Kansas, and soon he, too, was collecting the imprints of Late Cretaceous leaves from the Dakota sandstone exposed near the ranch where they lived. His father did not consider fossil collecting a suitable occupation for a young man, but Charles persisted in his interests. In 1870, he packaged up a set of fossils collected by himself and his older brother and shipped them to the Smithsonian Institution. The fossils drew the attention of noted paleobotanist Leo Lesquereux, who traveled to Kansas to meet Charles Sternberg

The Sternbergs were a pioneering family of Kansas fossil finders. Below is their family tree:

LEVI STERNBERG *(1814–1896)*

|--GEORGE M. STERNBERG *(1833–1915)*

|--CHARLES H. STERNBERG *(1850–1943)*

|--GEORGE F. STERNBERG *(1883–1969)*

|--CHARLES M. STERNBERG *(1885–1981)*

|--LEVI STERNBERG *(1894–1976)*

WEBLINK

Discover more about the Sternberg family at the official Sea Monsters website.

THE STERNBERG FINDS

7-27. Collecting leaf Nodules. Near Carnerio. Ellsworth Kansas.

Shown here in 1927, George F. Sternberg searches for fossilized leaves. Sternberg collected and studied many different forms of life from prehistoric Kansas.

CALLED BY MANY A GREAT "DINOSAUR DYNASTY," five Sternbergs across two generations made paleontology history in the western plains of Kansas during the late 19th and early 20th century. Levi Sternberg, the family patriarch, moved from New York to Iowa in 1865. His oldest son, George M., followed suit after medical school, traveling even farther West when he accepted a position as surgeon at Fort Harker, Kansas. Soon the rest of the family, including Levi's twin teenage sons, Charles and Edward, had joined George. George and his younger brother Charles were especially fascinated by the central Kansas landscape and the fossilized remains they were finding there. The Sternbergs began collecting leaf fossils—small rocks impressed over the ages with delicate vein-shaped imprints. Soon Charles had bags full of such specimens, which he eventually delivered to the Smithsonian Institution. In 1870, George M. relocated to New York, but by then Charles had dedicated himself to the study of fossils found in the Kansas chalk, not only leaf fossils but also the fossilized bones of ancient animals. He corresponded with scholars back East whose research involved the new field of paleontology. Darwin's theory of evolution was new and controversial. Discoveries from the field, such as the leaf and bone fossils that Charles Sternberg was collecting in Kansas, provided evidence for the new vision of an Earth on which unknown species trod and swam many millions of years before humankind.

Levi, youngest of Charles's three sons to become a fossil hunter

George F. Sternberg, left, with his father, Charles

George F. Sternberg's field journal, noting his October 1924 find of a tylosaur in Trego County, Kansas

The Sphinx, a distinctive rock formation in the Kansas chalk beds, proved fertile fossil hunting territory.

No-13-26

The "Sphinx"

George F. Sternberg's finds can be seen in the Sternberg Museum, established in the 1950s and named for him in 1970.

Fossil hunts meant camping adventures for Charles Sternberg and his three sons.

Soon Charles Sternberg married and began to raise a family of his own, who would join him on his fossil collecting trips to the field. Traveling and collecting, first by horse-drawn wagon and then by early automobile, the Sternberg family would camp for weeks in the dry Kansas flatlands, punctuated by the occasional remarkable chalk monument.

Each of Charles Sternberg's three sons—George F., Charles M., and Levi—contributed significantly to the family's fossil-finding business, whether by collecting, recording in words and images, or finding buyers for their discoveries. Father and sons developed new techniques for collecting the massive skeletons they were finding. Thanks to them and their innovative techniques, the remains of prehistoric sea monsters from western Kansas found their way to major museums in the United States and Europe where they can still be seen today. Word got around about the Sternbergs' field excursions and the remarkable bones they would find. People wanted to see for themselves, and occasionally small groups of people were visiting the Sternberg digs. Some stood and watched with wonder while others dug in, seeing if they could find a fossil in the Kansas chalk.

In the late 1920s, George F. Sternberg was invited to establish a museum in the locale where he and his family had been digging for decades. He became the resident paleontologist at the Kansas State Teachers College in Hays. There he began building the fossil collection of what is now called the Sternberg Museum at Fort Hays State University where sea monsters grace the walls.

BACKGROUND: *The Smoky Hill chalk of western Kansas, now dry, striated limestone, was once covered by a vast ocean, the Western Interior Sea, home to many of Earth's prehistoric marine reptiles.*

and explore the fossils of western Kansas himself. In 1872, Lesquereux published descriptions of many of the fossil leaves that the Sternberg brothers had found. He named one species, *Protophyllum sternbergi*, in honor of Charles Sternberg.

Charles remained in contact with Lesquereux for many years. His fossil leaf discoveries marked the beginning of the so-called Sternberg dynasty of American paleontology, a family of scientists whose discoveries shaped our understanding of the world of sea monsters that thrived in North America's Interior Sea many millions of years ago. Beginning in Kansas and later collecting fossils elsewhere in the United States, Canada, and Argentina, two generations of the Sternberg family established what has been called by many the Sternberg dynasty in the early years of American paleontology.

Their finds covered a wide range of species, not only marine reptiles but also sharks, a dinosaur, and giant mammals. They developed many of the modern techniques for the collection, preservation, and mounting of fossils, and the specimens they collected are still on display in museums around the world today.

PTERANODON STERNBERGI

Order: *Pterosauria*

Cretaceous Period • North America

Wingspan: 20 feet

FREELANCE FOSSIL FINDER

Charles Sternberg's big break came in 1876. A student at the Kansas State Agricultural College (now Kansas State University), he tried to join a fossil-hunting expedition led by Professor Mudge, Benjamin F. Mudge, Kansas's first state geologist. But Mudge, who was working for O. C. Marsh at the time, had more assistants than he needed. So Sternberg wrote a letter to Marsh's rival, Cope, offering his services as a fossil finder and requesting $300 to outfit an expedition. Cope wrote back, sending a check for the requested amount with a clear message: "Go to work." Sternberg purchased a team of ponies, hired a boy to drive them, and set out looking for fossils in western Kansas. He worked that way for the next four years, shipping a seemingly endless supply of specimens back East for Cope to study, identify, and describe.

Near the end of the first summer of fieldwork for Cope, Charles Sternberg came across a particularly productive canyon. There he discovered two mosasaur specimens, one on top of the other, separated by three feet of chalk. (Current research now indicates that although these two animals lay physically close together in the chalk, one died about 25,000 years before the other!) He also excavated a nearly complete specimen of a small mosasaur called *Clidastes*. By the end of the summer, Sternberg's

wagon was loaded with 800 pounds of fossil specimens. They were hauled across the prairie and loaded on the train for shipment to Philadelphia. That winter Sternberg went to Philadelphia, where he attended a meeting of the Academy of Natural Sciences and was introduced by Cope as the man who had collected the impressive fossils. For that, Sternberg received a generous round of applause.

As the 1877 field season began, O. C. Marsh asked his assistant, Samuel W. Williston, to pay close attention to what Sternberg was doing. The competition between Marsh and Cope was fierce and growing, and Marsh wanted to be sure he was not being outdone in the field. That July, Williston reported that Sternberg had shipped "1 bird, 19 pterodactyls, 38 saurians [mosasaurs], 5 turtles and 210 fishes, in all 15 boxes." One of those turtles was a fairly complete *Protostega gigas*, one of the largest turtles known to have inhabited the Western Interior Sea.

During four years of employment, Sternberg collected fossils in Kansas and elsewhere in the West, as directed by Cope. He never officially completed his college degree, but his experience in the field proved to be education enough. By 1880, Charles Sternberg felt confident enough about his knowledge and experience to write a brief paper, describing plant fossils he had collected from the Dakota sandstone. The following year he wrote another article, this one about the fossils of the Niobrara Group, a Cretaceous rock formation of chalk and shale named for the Niobrara River of Nebraska and Kansas. "These beds are of great value to science, as they contain the remains of animals that once inhabited the Cretaceous ocean," Sternberg wrote. "Perfect skeletons are found of huge saurians eighty feet in length. What a field for the imagination of the

In the Smithsonian National Museum of Natural History, the skeleton of a Late Cretaceous sea turtle, Protostega gigas, *shows its distinctive ribbed shell.*

student, to people the old Cretaceous seas with animals restored from their buried relics!"

Writing what amounted to the first article for popular readers about sea monsters, he took the liberty of picturing them dramatically. "I now in imagination walk the old Cretaceous beach; I hear the rush of mighty rivers, as, laden with the debris of the carboniferous hills, they pour into the ocean, depositing their loads of soft mud that is to cover and preserve the remains of animals living in these waters. Far out at sea, I observe a huge snake-like animal, with head erect, full twenty feet in the air, gazing into the depth below." Sternberg ended his article by crediting Cope, saying, "I hope he will pardon the use of some of his descriptions."

COLLECTING IN KANSAS

Seen in the film Sea Monsters, *these fossil-collecting tools (picks, hammers, brushes, and measuring sticks) resemble those carried by 19th-century paleontologists.*

In 1884 Sternberg's article, "Directions for Collecting Vertebrate Fossils," he took a realistic look at the hardships of fossil collecting in Kansas in those days. "The proper outfit for a collecting expedition consists of a good team of ponies or small mules, a light lumber wagon, cover, wall-tent, camp-stove or 'Dutch oven,' knives and forks, tin plates and cups, and other cooking-utensils," wrote Sternberg. "Each member of the party should be provided with a rubber blanket and coat, and a couple of pairs of woolen blankets; besides these but little extra baggage should be taken; a good pair of woolen shirts are valuable." He recommended "smoked glasses"—the 19th-century equivalent of sunglasses—for "collecting in hot weather."

Listing necessary tools, he mentioned "several small hand-picks, miner's-picks, with one point made into a duck-bill with sharp edge; butcher-knives, shovels and collecting-bags." The bags, he said, resembled "mail-carrier's bags, of heavy ducking, with two apartments—one for cotton, paper and string, and the other for fossils." To pack up the finds, Sternberg added, "there should always be kept on hand a supply of burlap sacks, old newspapers, cotton, manila paper and hop-needles; boxes and barrels for shipping."

He emphasized the need to keep accurate records—even though he and, later, his son George F. tended to remain somewhat secretive about the locations of their own choice finds. During the summer, Sternberg advised, one should plan to "go into the [Niobrara] beds early and work until ten o'clock, and in the afternoon leave camp at half past two and work as long as you can see." In this article, Sternberg's pioneering collection techniques are also discussed. He was among the first, for example, to champion the use of plaster of Paris in collecting fossils, noting that a good method of collecting small, fragile fossils of fish "is to cover the specimen with two or three inches of plaster of Paris and allow it to set, [since] this gives a fine protection to delicate bones." Sternberg would later adapt this method for collecting the massive remains of sea monsters from the Smoky Hill Chalk.

In the 1880s, Charles Sternberg settled down on a farm outside Lawrence, Kansas, where he and his wife raised four children. As each of their three boys—George F., Charles H., and Levi—got to be old enough, they joined their father in his work as a fossil finder. In 1891, Charles Sternberg made one of his major discoveries: a nearly complete specimen of a giant shark, *Cretoxyrhina mantelli*, commonly called a Ginsu shark. Although sharks are cartilaginous and do not have bones in the true sense, their cartilage can become calcified and thus be preserved as a fossil. In this case, the remains had been covered with limey mud on the sea bottom in a way that almost mummified them. The shark was a "full 25 feet long, with 250 teeth, chiefly in or near their original position," as Sternberg described it. His estimate of its length may be somewhat exaggerated, but the Ginsu was indeed

CRETOXYRHINA MANTELLI
Order: *Lamniformes*
Cretaceous Period • North America
25 feet

the largest shark that swam the Western Interior Sea during the time period represented by the depostition of the Smoky Hill chalk. In life, the Ginsu sharks must have approximated the modern great white shark in size, power, and predatory capability. Evidence suggests they fed on many kinds of prey, including large fish, plesiosaurs, and mosasaurs.

The specimen was shipped to Munich, where an American student, Charles Eastman, studied it for his doctoral dissertation. Before that time, the teeth of this prehistoric shark had been found individually, but a full set had never been collected all at once. Since its teeth had various shapes, paleontologists had ascribed them to seven different species. Sternberg's discovery proved that all the different-shaped teeth belonged to one animal. After Charles Sternberg's first discovery, more superb prehistoric shark remains were collected from the chalk, including an excellent specimen collected by his son George in 1965.

Over the years Charles Sternberg worked not only for E. D. Cope but also for his rival, O. C. Marsh, and then for Marsh's assistant, Samuel Williston, who became a professor of geology and paleontology at the University of Kansas. Sternberg worked under contract, finding fossils for museums far and wide as well, including the Palaeontological Museum of Munich, Germany, the Natural History Museum, at Tübingen University in Germany, the British Museum of Natural History and the Museum of Evolution, Uppsala, Sweden. Fossil finding was his life, so that even when no outside individual or organization paid his way, Charles Sternberg (and, soon, his sons) spent every season in western Kansas and elsewhere, hunting down evidence of its prehistory buried deep beneath the soil.

RIGHT: *Actors re-create George F. Sternberg's discovery of the head of a* Tylosaurus. *When Sternberg and his brothers first hunted fossils, Kansas was on the edge of the American frontier.*

OPPOSITE: *A* Xiphactinus *fish and a* Dolichorhychops *nearly collide as they both pursue a meal.*

LIKE FATHER, LIKE SONS

George F. Sternberg, Charles eldest son, started working for his father in the field when he was 13 years old. They began by collecting leaves in Ellsworth County near Fort Harker and worked their way west, eventually ending up in the Smoky Hill chalk. It was slow, difficult work, but George enjoyed it, and the two made a good team.

In the summer of 1900, Charles and George F. Sternberg made one of their most important discoveries. As George F., by then 17, searched the rocks in Logan County, western Kansas, he came across the remains of a small plesiosaur. The bones were scattered and fragile, but the specimen appeared to be nearly complete. Even the skull was intact. Father and son spent two weeks removing the nearly 500 pounds of chalk matrix that contained the bones. They sent the specimen to the University of Kansas, where it was cleaned and mounted. They had discovered a new species, soon named *Dolichorhynchops osborni*, a relatively small, short-necked plesiosaur measuring about 10 feet in length with a narrow skull, 2 feet long, and a jaw with many sharp teeth. The Sternbergs had discovered and collected the most complete plesiosaur skeleton found in the United States up until that time.

As winter approached in 1901, the Sternberg team, father and son, discovered a nearly complete skeleton of a giant predatory fish now called *Xiphactinus audax*. Although the species had been known from fragmentary remains since the 1870s, a complete fish had never been collected. Cold weather was setting in, and the Sternbergs had to beat the coming winter in order to collect the specimen. Using the method Charles Sternberg had perfected of collecting fossils in large slabs of plaster of Paris, they built box frames around the specimen and poured in the plaster. In such cold weather, the plaster set up slowly and then froze solid as they worked to get the specimens out of the ground. They finally removed three wood-framed boxes of plaster and chalk containing the specimen, each box weighing over 600 pounds. Through hard work and tremendous patience, Charles Sternberg and his sons excavated the specimen and sent it to the American Museum of Natural History in New York. Measuring almost 16 feet, the Sternberg's *Xiphactinus* fossil was one of the best examples of a large fossil fish anywhere in the world at the time.

Soon George Sternberg's younger brothers, Charlie and Levi, had joined their brother and father in the work of fossil finding. During the summer of 1906, Charlie discovered one of the most complete and well-preserved fossils ever collected of *Hesperornis regalis*, a large, flightless bird with teeth. Although missing a skull, the

HESPERORNIS REGALIS

Order: Hesperorithiformes

Cretaceous Period • North America

6.5 feet

remains were laid out in a posture very close to the way the animal would have looked in life. A marine bird of the Cretaceous period, *Hesperornis* swam the same seas as the plesiosaurs and mosasaurs. It may have behaved like a modern penguin, hunting small fish and invertebrates. Charles H. Sternberg dubbed it the "snake-bird of the Niobrara" for its long, flexible neck.

George F. Sternberg developed a special talent in photography, documenting the fossils found by his family and using the photos to advertise specimens they wanted to sell. Although we do not have his field notes, photos taken of specimens he collected during the 1907 field season, for example, show how well he did at finding fossils. One photo shows young George F. working in the middle of a large chalk exposure, his wagon and team of horses in the background, at the ready to haul his discoveries away. Others show some of his finds for the summer: the skull and lower jaws of a pteranodon and the skulls of two examples of the predatory fish *Xiphactinus*.

In 1918, the Sternbergs were back in Kansas, working together to collect fossils from the chalk. On his second day back in Kansas, Charles found the remains of a large *Tylosaurus* eroding out along Butte Creek in Logan County. He and his sons

George F. Sternberg, at left, counted the fish-within-a-fish that he collected in 1952 as one of his greatest finds. Here, unidentified friends and their children admire the remarkable double fossil.

meticulously worked to expose the remains. When the skeleton was uncovered, it turned out to be nearly complete, missing only about six feet of its tail and small parts of its hind limbs. It was an impressive *Tylosaurus* specimen. More importantly, however, it contained within its body cavity the partially digested bones of a juvenile polycotylid plesiosaur, probably a *Dolichorhynchops*. It was the first evidence that mosasaurs preyed on plesiosaurs—a find that was announced by Charles later that year, but received little notice in the scientific community. The *Tylosaurus* specimen was quickly mounted as a museum exhibit but the remains of its last meal was stored away in the collection. It wasn't until the plesiosaur remains were rediscovered in 2001 that Charles Sternberg finally received the credit for this truly unique specimen from the Late Cretaceous monster-eat-monster world.

In 1925, George F. Sternberg's discoveries included the remains of nine turtles, including a partial *Protostega*, and a *Xiphactinus audax* almost 12 feet long. He eventually sold them to the organization that became the Smithsonian National Museum of Natural History. Visible within the ribs of the huge predatory fish fossil were the partially digested vertebrae of a smaller fish. It was the first of several fish-within-a-fish specimens that he would discover, important fossil evidence for the dietary habits of animals in the Late Cretaceous seas. Several months later, George F. received a letter from Charles Gilmore at the United States National Museum. Gilmore indicated that they had nearly completed work mounting the *Protostega*

Opening its mouth wide, a Tylosaurus *grabs and swallows whole a juvenile* Dolichorhynchops.

skeleton and that they had found parts of the skull of the fish inside the *Xiphactinus* specimen when it was being prepared. He also wrote that he was "very much pleased with the entire transaction."

George F. Sternberg recovered his most famous "fish within a fish" specimen in 1952. In the spring of that year, a group from the American Museum of Natural History were on a field trip with Sternberg when one of them discovered a fossilized fish fin. Unable to extend their time in the field, the students left it to Sternberg to excavate the entire fossil. After weeks of careful excavation in the hot Kansas sun, Sternberg and his team revealed one of the most complete *Xiphactinus* ever found. Even more remarkable was that the big fish's last meal, a smaller, six-foot-long fish called *Gillicus arcuatus*, was found perfectly preserved inside.

Fish remains are among the most common vertebrate fossils found in the Smoky Hill Chalk, but specimens as complete as this one are fairly rare. An interesting trait amoung *Xiphactinus* specimens is that a high percentage of them have been found with *Gillicus* remains inside. A giant, 17-foot specimen found in 1996 contained a partially digested *Gillicus*, and the Denver Museum of Nature and Science also has a similar fossil. The relatively frequent discovery of *Xiphactinus* who had eaten shortly before death has led scientists to speculate that the last meal could have been the cause of death. In the Sternberg fossil, perhaps a *Gillicus* fin pierced the heart or a major blood vessel of the larger fish, causing it to expire quickly.

George F. Sternberg's digs became something of a local attraction. When he publicized locally that he was working to excavate a huge fossil "over 30 cars [came] out on Sunday, wagons and riders, to see the specimen. I believe over 150 people," Sternberg wrote in his notes. "There were 17 cars here at one time and they kept coming until dark." A month later he found another big *Xiphactinus*, and it was purchased by the local school system. This specimen is still on display at the Fick Fossil and History Museum in Oakley, Kansas.

For much of the 20th century the Sternbergs continued exploring the fossil landscape of the Western Interior Sea. They collected and preserved the remains of hundreds of organisms from earlier times. Their decades of discoveries fill in many details about life on Earth during the Late Cretaceous period. Thanks to the undaunted energy and careful collecting techniques of the Sternberg dynasty, museums all over the world now display the fossils that they found, helping us to picture and appreciate life in the unfathomable Late Cretaceous underwater world.

Re-created for the film are George Sternberg's notes of a remarkable mosasaur find: a Tylosaurus *with* Dolichorhynchops *remains on the inside.*

Before swimming in the deep open waters of the Western Interior Sea, Dolichorhynchops *began their lives in the coastal regions, where their mothers migrated to give birth.*

S HALLOW WATERS WERE A SAFE HAVEN FOR many sea creatures of the Late Cretaceous period. Larger predators roamed the deeper waters, so many creatures took to the shallows for its protection. Slower swimmers, like the long-necked *Styxosaurus*, above and below opposite, probably stayed close to the shallows all year round. There they could avoid these larger, faster predators. Styxosaurs were successful hunters themselves; their long necks allowed them to sneak up on their prey. The *Dolichorhynchops*, above opposite, visited the coastal waters and migrated there before giving birth to their young. While these short-necked plesiosaurs were young, they most likely remained in the shallows with the safety of their mothers' protection. As long as food was plentiful, they may have remained there. But as their prey migrated to deeper waters, the dollies would eventually have to leave to follow their food.

Styxosaurus teeth were
sharp like needles rather
than serrated. It made
them ideal for seizing fish
but not for tearing flesh.
They probably swallowed
their prey whole.

GLASSES OFF
FOR NEXT PAGE

CHAPTER THREE

IN DANGEROUS
WATERS

A female mosasaur considers a shark, Cretoxyrhina mantelli, *as fit food to share with her offspring, swimming behind her.*

F WE COULD IMAGINE OURSELVES BACK 82 MILLION YEARS, TO THE waters of the vast inland sea that covered the central portion of the developing continent of North America toward the end of the Cretaceous period, we would be witnessing one of the most dangerous times and places ever known on this planet. On the land, ferocious meat-eating theropods roamed in search of prey, while reptilian pterosaurs spread their wings and soared above in the skies. But in the vast waters below, an incredible array of marine animals lived in the shallows and depths. Some huge and voracious, others delicate and vulnerable—they all interacted in an underwater drama in which the early evolution of reptiles, fish, birds, and other creatures played itself out.

The film *Sea Monsters* takes viewers into this dangerous world as it follows the life of a plesiosaur called *Dolichorhynchops*, "dolly" for short. The life of this sea monster begins in the shallows of the Western Interior Sea when an

DOLICHORHYNCHOPS OSBORNI
Order: *Plesiosauria*
Cretaceous Period • North America
15 feet

LEFT: *A plesiosaur, called* Dolichorhynchops, *grabs a fish in the waters of the Western Interior Sea, 82 million years ago.*

THE SEA MONSTERS' TALE

The film follows the adventures of a young Dolichorhynchops in the Western Interior Sea.

NEW LIVES

Plot Point: A male and female DOLICHORHYNCHOPS are born 82 million years ago.
Setting: Shallows of the Western Interior Sea

SAFE HAVEN

Plot Point: The twin dollies stay with their mother and live with other creatures, like the STYXOSAURUS.
Setting: Shallows of the Western Interior Sea

DEEPER WATER

Plot Point: Following a migrating ENCHODUS school, the mother and twins leave the shallows.
Setting: Open Water of the Western Interior Sea

TERRIBLE LOSS

Plot Point: A CRETOXYRINA shark kills the mother dolly, leaving the twins alone.
Setting: Open Water of the Western Interior Sea

NARROW ESCAPE

Plot Point: The female dolly evades a shark but sustains a minor injury, a shark's tooth embedded in her flipper.
Setting: Open Water of the Western Interior Sea

The Dolichorhynchops *survives a vicious shark attack but escapes with a wound.*

The embedded tooth in her flipper is a permanent mark of her encounter.

adult female gives birth to two young, a male and a female. As soon as these two are born, instinct draws them up to the surface of the water for their first breaths. These animals may live in the water, but, like their land-dwelling evolutionary ancestors, they must breathe air.

At first, the young dollies stay close to their mother for protection as they are too small and vulnerable to face the dangers of the deeper, open waters. Other animals share the dollies' shallow birthing grounds: ammonites, a sort of squid in a shell found abundantly in these prehistoric waters; *Hesperornis,* a flightless bird with sharp teeth; *Styxosaurus,* a long-necked variety of plesiosaur which, like the dollies, comes into the shallows to give birth.

As the dollies mature, they move out into deeper waters, following a migrating school of fish. Dangers lurk all around as the twin dollies make their way through the deep waters of the inland sea. Large predatory fish, like *Xiphactinus,* hunt in the open waters for other fish. Cruising alongside them in these waters are prehistoric sharks, including the *Cretoxyrhina* (or Ginsu shark), whose rows of razor-sharp teeth can rip through the flesh and bones of a plesiosaur. The unchallenged ruler is the *Tylosaurus,* a massive mosasaur at the top of the food chain.

No human being ever witnessed a Late Cretaceous life story like this one, of course. The knowledge that goes into the making of a film such as *Sea Monsters* arises out of decades of

The twin dollies break the water's surface to take a breath. Like land-dwelling reptiles, sea monsters do not have gills and must breathe air.

collection, preparation, and study of the many marine fossils found buried in the rocks of the Late Cretaceous. As paleontologists around the world share their finds, bone by bone, discovery by discovery, the collected evidence helps us to re-create their world as it may have been. It is because of their scientific collections and detailed analysis that we are able to imagine the drama, the possibilities, and the adventures of the sea monsters' world and the wide variety of fascinating creatures that inhabited it.

THE INVERTEBRATES

Untold billions of small invertebrates thrived in the Western Interior Sea, feeding on the sea's abundance of single-celled plankton and in turn providing food for larger predators. Small organisms fed on photosynthetic, algae-like nannoplankton. Sardine-sized fish ate fish larvae and small invertebrates; the small fish were in turn eaten by larger fish such as *Gillicus* or *Bananogmius*. These predators became the prey of even larger fish—*Xiphactinus,* for example—or of Ginsu sharks and mosasaurs.

Deeper waters supported other invertebrates, like crinoids and cephalopods. Crinoids were prehistoric echinoderms, the same phylum of today's today's starfish and sea urchins. Only one form of echinoderm fossil has been found in the Smoky Hill chalk, an unusual form called *Uintacrinus.* In 1917, Charles Sternberg himself described these crinoids as "about the shape of half an egg, with an opening in the center, and ten arms radiating from the margin. These arms were three feet long, with feathered edges."

As a group, cephalopods had already existed for more than 200 million years by the Late Cretaceous, by which time several different types, ancestors of the modern squid and octopus, were flourishing. Some, like the ammonites and the baculites, bore shells; others, like the giant squids, did not. Ammonites, now extinct, looked like a squid living inside a coiled and sometimes intricately ornamented shell. They could grow quite large; some ammonite shells found from the Late Cretaceous measure up to three feet across. Their shells included a chamber that contained air. An ammonite propelled itself through the water by expelling a jet of water out of its body. Like today's squid, they had sharp, beak-like jaws located inside a ring of tentacles, which they used to capture their prey, small fish and other cephalopods. Smaller cephalopods with similar motor and predatory habits also inhabited the Western Interior Sea, including scaphites, which had small spiral shells, and baculites, which had straight shells.

GILLICUS ARCUATUS
Order: *Ichthyodectiformes*
Cretaceous Period • North America
6 feet

BELOW: *The spindly arms of two fossilized crinoids, called* Uintacrinus, *are visible in this specimen from the Kansas chalk.*

Shellless cephalopods also shared the waters with the dollies and other sea monsters of that time. *Tusoteuthis,* the giant squid of the Late Cretaceous, was probably similar in appearance and behavior to the giant squids of today. With their 10 tentacles stretched out, they may have reached lengths of 25 to 35 feet. They fed on anything they could capture with their tentacles, mostly smaller cephalopods and fish. They may have preyed upon small marine reptiles, but they spent most of their time farther below the surface than mosasaurs and plesiosaurs would have dived. Like ammonites, they moved (backwards!) by expelling a jet of water through a siphon on the lower part of their bodies. They had already developed the defense mechanism used today by modern squid: When attacked, they could squirt a dark, murky fluid out into the water, blinding or confusing their enemies long enough so they could escape.

Since these squid were soft-bodied animals, with neither an outer shell nor an internal skeleton, few traces of them can be found in the fossil record. The one hard internal structure that sometimes survives to the present day is the paddle-shaped rachis, or squid pen, made of chitin. Occasionally these structures are preserved among other fossils and may show the bite marks of a predator that attacked and killed the squid.

EARLY WATER BIRDS

In 1871, O. C. Marsh collected the remains of a large flightless bird, which he named *Hesperornis regalis. Hesperornis,* which could reach five feet in length, had a slender, snake-like neck that it held above water as it swam, striking a silhouette something like that of a grebe of the present day. Its feeding and nesting habits may have been much like those of the modern penguin. But curiously, whereas penguins today inhabit only the Southern Hemisphere, the remains of *Hesperornis* and other related species have been discovered only in the Northern Hemisphere. In fact, specimens are much more common north of Kansas, especially in Canada, which may indicate that, like penguins, these flightless birds preferred cooler water.

While they would not have been able to fly or to stand on land, these birds were strong underwater swimmers. Unlike the penguin, which uses its wings to literally fly underwater, *Hesperornis* used its large, well-developed hind limbs and webbed feet to swim. The bird's small, rudimentary wings clung close to its body, suggesting that these appendages were too small to be of use. Its flattened tail may have served as a diving plane, helping the bird to change depth and direction under water. We assume

Saying these creatures' names can be a mouthful. Below is a quick pronunciation guide to sound out their names:

DOLICHORHYNCHOPS = *dol-ee-ko-ring-kopz*

ELASMOSAUR = *ee-lass'-moh-sor*

HESPERORNIS = *hez-pe-rorn-uhs*

MOSASAUR = *mohz-uh-sor*

PLESIOSAUR = *plez-ee'-oh-sor*

PLIOSAUR = *plee-oh-sor*

STYXOSAURUS = *sticks-oh-sor-uhs*

TUSOTEUTHIS = *too-so-too-thuhs*

TYLOSAURUS = *tie-lo-sor-uhs*

XIPHACTINUS = *zi-fak-tin-uhs*

by its toothed jaw that the *Hesperornis* snatched bite-sized prey like fish and other sea creatures. But it was a creature-eat-creature world, which also means that this hunting bird could also become prey, as shown in the remains of a large *Tylosaurus* found in South Dakota, whose stomach contents included a *Hesperornis*.

FINNED PREDATORS, FINNED PREY

Fish were abundant in the Late Cretaceous seas, both as predators and prey. One of the primary food fish of the Late Cretaceous oceans was named *Enchodus* and is a distant relative of modern salmon. Some species of *Enchodus* were as small as a sardine, while others grew up to four feet long. All *Enchodus*, small and large, came equipped with fangs. They must have used such long, slender teeth, prominent at the front of their upper and lower jaws, for trapping smaller prey. Paleontologists believe that *Enchodus* probably congregated and swam together in large schools, like herrings, sardines, or anchovies. Just about everything in the ocean preyed on them. Some predators may have herded them into densely compacted formations, termed "bait balls." A predator simply swam through a mass of small fish with its mouth wide open, gorging itself on all it could hold.

There is no doubt that the long, torpedo-shaped *Xiphactinus* was the top predator among the bony fishes of its day. Growing to a length of at least 18 feet, these fish were long, slender, and speedy, like tarpons on steroids. Their jaws held teeth up to

A Hesperornis *dives down in pursuit of prey. Scientists believe it relied on its strong legs and webbed feet to swim.*

Searching for food, this group of Dolichorhynchops *swims out to the more dangerous open waters. The lowest depths of the Western Interior Sea were no more than 600 feet.*

3 inches long, and their mouths opened wide enough to swallow 6- to 7-foot prey. Perhaps their eagerness to eat large fish got them into trouble, for more than a dozen specimens of *Xiphactinus* have been discovered with only partially digested remains of a meal inside, as if the creature had died shortly after as it gulped down its last, big meal. The most famous such find was George Sternberg's famous fish-within-a-fish, the 13-foot *Xiphactinus* containing an entire, 6-foot-long fish skeleton inside.

Another ominous predatory fish of those seas, *Protosphyraena perniciosa*, would have looked like a modern billfish or marlin. The skull and pectoral fins of *Protosphyraena* are common fossils in the chalk but complete skeletons are rare. Scientists speculate that once the fish had died, either scavengers quickly tore it apart, or else the corpse drifted until it rotted and fell apart, dropping the fins here, the tail there, and the skull someplace else. One recent find finally provided a complete specimen, which now confirms more details about this strange fish. This creature had a sharp snout out of which protruded blade-like teeth, all facing forward like a dagger poised to thrust. As if that weren't enough, its long, bony fin had a sawtooth edge, whose exact purpose is still under debate.

PROTOSPHYRAENA

Order: *Perciformes*

Cretaceous Period • North America

6 feet

SHARKS OF THE INLAND SEAS

Two types of shark were common in the middle of the Western Interior Sea during this part of the Late Cretaceous: the Ginsu shark and the crow shark. While distinctly different in size and habits, these two sharks may have eaten the same kinds of food. Fossils show tooth marks from both types of shark, suggesting that they may have attacked together, shared their prey, or stolen their prey from each other.

The larger and more dangerous of the two was *Cretoxyrhina mantelli*, the Ginsu shark. Ginsu sharks grew up to 20 or more feet in length, similar to a modern great white shark. Nicknamed after a brand of kitchen knife renowned for its slicing and dicing abilities, this shark used a mouth full of razor-sharp, bone-shearing teeth to capture, kill, and consume its prey. Ginsu sharks likely fed on smaller mosasaurs and other marine reptiles just as great whites go after seals and small whales today. Researchers often find stray remains of mosasaurs and plesiosaurs, suggesting that the animals had been torn apart, partially digested, and then regurgitated by Ginsu sharks. Sometimes telltale fragments of Ginsu shark teeth remain embedded in the sea monsters' fossilized bones. Severed vertebrae more than 2 inches in diameter offer testimony to the tremendous force behind a Ginsu's bite. One specimen, a 9-vertebrae portion of a dinosaur tail, evoked the scene of a Ginsu shark so powerful it could bite off a 20-inch section and swallow it whole.

The crow sharks (*Squalicorax*) were smaller, about one-third the length of the largest Ginsu sharks. Judging from the thousands of teeth that have been found, paleontologists believe that the crow was the more common of the two shark species. Like many modern sharks, these animals played a critical role in the ecology of the Western Interior Sea. It appears that they were primarily scavengers, stripping the flesh off the bones of dead animals and thus recycling biological materials. Their teeth were much smaller than those of *Cretoxyrhina*, with edges serrated like a steak knife, an ideal design for tearing flesh. The marks of Crow shark teeth were found on many fossilized bones. It is rare, in fact, to find fossils of large vertebrates in the chalk —birds, pteranodons, fish, plesiosaurs, mosasaurs, even Ginsu sharks—without serrated bite marks somewhere on the bones, probably from crow sharks.

Sharks and sea monsters vied for dominance in the Late Cretaceous oceans. The record tells us that as mosasaurs evolved, they fed on all kinds of prey— possibly they dined on baby sharks. We know that modern sharks are unable to reproduce fast enough to sustain losses due to predation by humans; perhaps Cretaceous sharks faced similar pressures due to aggressive predation by mosasaurs. As the end of the Late Cretaceous period neared, mosasaurs had reached their peak of size and dominance, but the Ginsu sharks had already disappeared.

SQUALICORAX
Order: *Lamniformes*
Cretaceous Period • North America
6 feet

HARD-SHELLED SURVIVORS

Only one group of seagoing marine reptiles escaped extinction at the end of the Cretaceous period: the marine turtles. Some prehistoric species, notably *Protostega gigas*, were truly huge, growing more than ten feet long, but most were quite similar in size to the green, loggerhead, and leatherback turtles living in the oceans of today. Unlike the other large marine reptiles, even the hugest of the marine turtles of the Western Interior Sea did not completely sever their ties to life on land. They were able to exist on shore. Their kind has survived through millennia when ichthyosaurs, then plesiosaurs, and mosasaurs failed to do so.

Most species of marine turtles, like turtleshells of the present day, have a carapace, or upper shell, made of expanded and fused bones that form a relatively solid dome. In the case of the giant *Protostega,* however, the shell looked more like the rafters of a roof, with large spaces in between the bones. The name *Protostega* reflects this roof-like appearance: It means, literally, "first roof." This configuration of bones confused early paleontologists, who did not associate it with other turtles, but we now know that this same structure can be found in the modern-day leatherback turtle.

Marine turtles of the Late Cretaceous, unlike sea monsters, kept their ties to life on land. They reproduced by laying eggs there. Since female turtles left the water and came ashore seasonally, their limbs had to retain a certain amount of flexibility in order to support and move their bodies on land. Even so, the immense weight of these animals may have presented a problem when on land: An adult female *Protostega,* it is estimated, might have weighed a ton or more, which made dragging her body out of the ocean to lay eggs a challenge. Well-adapted to living in the fairly constant temperature of the ocean, these turtles would have been unable to adjust to the heat of the sun on land. Their terrestrial egg-laying practice clearly placed significant evolutionary restrictions on the species.

Laying eggs on the beach left turtles vulnerable to predators, too. Then as now, leaving a large clutch of eggs behind in a shallow beach nest was an invitation

At home in the water, the giant turtle Protostega *still had to drag its heavy body ashore to lay eggs. Scientists speculate that it could weigh about a ton.*

to any number of land animals looking for an easy meal. Even if they were not discovered during their incubation period, the multitudes of baby sea turtles hatching simultaneously along a beachfront would certainly attract hungry predators. Many newborn turtles would have been eaten as they manuevered down the sand toward the water. Once in the ocean, many more would have died in the jaws of large fish, sharks, and mosasaurs. While the marine turtle's reproductive strategy seems risky, it may also have been the secret to their survival. With such a large number of baby turtles hatching all at the same time, at least some survived and matured in each generation. There was, and is, safety in numbers.

Unfortunately, no marine turtle specimens have been found with preserved stomach contents, so we cannot be certain about what they were eating. We assume their diet consisted of similar foods that modern sea turtles consume: jellyfish, invertebrates like squid or crab, and some fish. Their sharp beaks and strong jaws would have been useful in eating a variety of things. They may have scavenged the carcasses of dead animals floating on the sea surface. Most likely they were opportunists, able to eat just about anything that was available. Dietary opportunism was another evolutionary advantage.

Some of the *Protostega* specimens discovered to date are reasonably complete, but some are missing limbs and skulls—a sign that perhaps the remains of these giant turtles were scavenged by sharks or other predators. Specimens have been collected with deep shark bite marks on the limb bones and carapace, and broken tips of shark teeth have been found embedded in other bones, all indicating that Ginsu sharks preyed on turtles. The smaller turtles, including juvenile *Protostega*, were bite-sized meals for a sea monster. Not many of these smaller turtles died of old age, and few of their remains have been preserved intact.

PROTOSTEGA GIGAS

Order: *Testudines*

Cretaceous Period • North America

10 feet

SHORT-NECKED SEA MONSTERS

In the film *Sea Monsters*, we follow the adventures of a short-necked plesiosaur, the *Dolichorhynchops osborni*, called "dolly" in the movie. Thanks to the Sternbergs and others, we have several relatively complete specimens of this species of polycotylid,

or short-necked plesiosaur. In fact, of all the plesiosaurs of the Western Interior Sea, the dolly is best represented among paleontological remains.

The earliest ancestors of *Dolichorhynchops* left the land and entered the oceans during the Triassic period, up to 250 million years ago. Then smaller, lizard-like animals called nothosaurs lived along the water's edge and hunted for prey in shallow water. Although they could swim, they still had functional legs for crawling ashore. Over millennia, some nothosaurs became fully adapted to life in the ocean. These animals were the earliest of the plesiosaurs and shared the oceans—and available prey—with the ichthyosaurs for millions of years. From these animals evolved the plesiosaurs of the Late Cretaceous. One species of big-headed plesiosaurs called pliosaurs died out around 95 million years ago. Others, though—both the short-necked species, also called polycotylids, and the long-necked species, called elasmosaurs—evolved and survived through to the end of the Late Cretaceous.

By about 82 million years ago, these short-necked plesiosaurs had evolved to a length of 12 to 15 feet, head to tail. Their heads were unusually elongated, much like those of the slender-snouted crocodiles we call gavials today, and their long jaws were filled with 30 to 40 sharp teeth in a single row. While modern mammals, including humans (and even giraffes), have only 7 cervical, or neck, vertebrae, the dolly had 20.

The configuration of the *Dolichorhynchops*'s tooth-filled jaw suggests that these animals preyed on small fish by slashing their heads sideways. Slender and pointed, these were teeth good for grabbing but not cutting. Dollies likely swallowed their prey whole, yet the narrowness of their skull and their long, protruding jaws would have limited the size of animals they could grab. They probably had to eat large numbers of small prey to get the energy they needed.

Dolichorhynchops and other short-necked plesiosaurs also had large eyes, which must have aided them in locating their prey in dimly lit waters. Aside from that, we know relatively little about their senses. There is no evidence to indicate that they had external ears, but their inner ears, providing a sense of balance, must have been well developed in order for them to swim and hunt effectively in their three-dimensional underwater environment. Some research suggests that plesiosaurs detected their prey by scent, directing a flow of water in through their nostrils and out the corners of their mouth while swimming. This is still only conjecture, however. Dollies probably primarily hunted by sight and lived much like modern porpoises, feeding on the

ABOVE: *The big eyes and long snout of this* Dolichorhynchops bonneri *resemble those of its relative* Dolichorhynchops osbourni (*who lived 4 million years before*).

OPPOSITE: *The dolly's long snout and pointy teeth indicates that it hunted by slashing its head sideways to snatch small fish. Its narrow jaws held anywhere from 30 to 40 sharp teeth.*

abundance of small fish and cephalopods like ammonites and squid in the shallow coastal waters.

The fossil record only hints at the outward appearance of the dollies. Paleontologists study the bones and then they envision the flesh and skin that must have covered them. We presume that these sea monsters had a smooth, not scaly, skin covering their bodies. Although we have no idea what color they were, they were most likely a dark color above and a light color underneath, the combination observed fairly consistently in modern-day fish and marine mammals, such as swordfish and killer whales.

The shoulder and pelvic girdles connected to the spine and served as attachment points for the broad sheets of muscles with which they moved their limbs. Each of the dolly's four paddles was constructed of almost a hundred bones, fitting tightly together like the interlocking pieces of a puzzle. This sturdy set of limbs would have been too stiff to use on land, but it had evolved into a design that provided excellent underwater aerodynamics.

All indications are that the *Dolichorhynchops* moved through the water not by pumping its limbs like the oars of a rowboat but by holding them out flat and using them like the wings of a bird to fly through the water. In cross-section, the dolly's limbs were shaped much like the wings of an airplane, with a thick leading edge, a curved upper surface, and thin trailing edge. The tips of these limbs may have flexed slightly as the animal swam through the water, reducing turbulence and improving

A mother Dolichorhynchops *delivers the first of her twins. The fossil record indicates that these sea monsters bore live young and traveled to shallow waters to give birth.*

efficiency, much like the winglets on a modern jet. The four limbs moved down together to generate lift, pulling the plesiosaur's body forward and effectively allowing it to soar though the water. Minor adjustments in stroke and deflection would have allowed the swimming animal to change direction or make quick turns, just like those that can be observed in the underwater flight of today's penguins.

DOLICHORHYNCHOPS ▶ fossil remains have demonstrated that plesiosaurs gave birth to live young: Fossils of unborn young have been found inside a mother's body cavity. Dollies probably carried two or three relatively large babies at one time. In the animal world, larger size at birth generally means a better chance of survival for the individual, an alternative to the strategy of sea turtles, which laid as many as a hundred small eggs at one time, in effect betting that a few would reach adulthood. Birth size alone is no guarantee of survival, however, because during the age of sea monsters, larger predators always lurked nearby, ready to make a meal of any smaller animal they could catch.

We suspect that in the case of the plesiosaurs, the mothers and young may have stayed together as a family group while the babies gained in size. Parental oversight and protection is observable in many groups of animals, from fish to amphibians to reptiles—some snakes and alligators—to birds. That being said, however, no real evidence has been found for or against the notion that plesiosaurs lived together in groups like some marine mammals today. Very few remains of adult and baby plesiosaurs have been collected in association.

Short-necked plesiosaurs such as *Dolichorhynchops* probably had few enemies, but those they did have were ferocious predators. Evidence of predation on plesiosaurs by sharks, particularly the large Ginsu sharks, is fairly rare in the chalk, but this may be because plesiosaur remains themselves are rare. Often partially digested bones are found, which probably represent material regurgitated by large sharks. Most often, these remains include small upper limb bones, suggesting that juvenile plesiosaurs were attacked and dismembered, but occasionally they include other skeletal elements from adults. It is also likely that the bigger marine reptiles, mosasaurs, fed on plesiosaurs when they could catch them. One historic discovery revealed a large *Tylosaurus* skeleton with the remains of a juvenile plesiosaur preserved inside. The mosasaur had apparently died within a couple of days of eating the plesiosaur, before the devoured animal's bones were entirely digested.

WEBLINK ▶

Discover more about the *Dolichorhynchops* at the official Sea Monsters website.

The actor portraying Charles F. Sternberg carefully excavates the soil surrounding a massive Tylosaurus *skull.*

HEADS OR TAILS?

ABOVE: *Fossils often leave questions unanswered about the configuration of the living animal. Paleontologist E. D. Cope put the head on the wrong end when he reconstructed* Elasmosaurus *remains found in Kansas in 1867.*

IN THE LATE 1860s, E. D. Cope, then a young paleontologist in Philadelphia, opened crates that had been shipped to him by rail from the frontier plains. Inside were hundreds of pounds of fossil remains, excavated by Theophilus H. Turner, a surgeon at Fort Wallace, who discovered them in the Pierre Shale of Kansas in 1867.

After reassembling the bones, Cope announced on March 24, 1869, the discovery of a new prehistoric marine reptile to the Academy of Natural Sciences. He named the creature *Elasmosaurus platyurus,* literally "flat-tailed plate reptile." Later that year Cope published his findings and, at his own expense, printed bulletins with his announcement, including a drawing of the skeleton that resembled a modern-day lizard, Cope's academic specialty, with a short neck and a long tail. In another drawing, published in early 1870, Cope added flesh and skin to the creature, still envisioned with the same short neck and long tail.

In these bulletins, Cope proudly shared these findings with many of his friends and professional acquaintances in the United States and Europe. However, in March 1870, his mentor, Joseph Leidy, announced to the Academy of Natural Sciences that Cope had "described the skeleton in a reversed position to the true one." The elasmosaur's head was placed on the wrong end of the vertebral column. In other words, Cope had put the skeleton together backwards.

Joseph Leidy's correct configuration of the *Elasmosaurus*

E. D. Cope's first—and incorrect—configuration

Providing access to the places where fossils were found, the Kansas Pacific Railroad came to Fort Hays, Kansas, in 1867.

Joseph Leidy (1823–1891)

O. C. Marsh (1832–1899)

E. D. Cope (1840–1897)

Soldiers and their surgeon, Theophilus H. Turner (standing at left) at Fort Wallace, Kansas in the 1860s

Cope recognized his mistake and set about to recall as many of the bulletins as he could. He promised to send a corrected version back to the owner of every one he reclaimed. Most copies of the erroneous publication were returned, but a few were not and managed to survive to this day. One of them ended up in the hands of Cope's rival, O. C. Marsh. He retained a copy, which still remains in the collection of the Peabody Museum at Yale University.

Almost 20 years later, Marsh claimed in a newspaper story that he was the one who had informed Cope that *Elasmosaurus* was assembled backwards and that was why Cope had been "his bitter enemy" ever since. However, the written record shows that it was Joseph Leidy who discovered the error and brought it to Cope's attention. In fact, Marsh did not mention it in print until he made a brief comment in 1873, noting that "after investigating a very perfect specimen for months, [Cope] placed *the head on the end of the tail*, and restored the animal in this position."

The controversy over Cope's head-on-the-wrong-end reconstruction of the plesiosaur remains tended to overshadow the importance of the specimen. Dr. Turner died at Fort Wallace in 1869 before getting the credit he deserved for his discovery.

LONG-NECKED SEA MONSTERS

Elasmosaurs (literally "ribbon reptiles") were plesiosaurs with extremely long necks, strange-looking animals by any standards. The first Europeans who unearthed plesiosaur remains described the creature as a "serpent threaded through the shell of a turtle." To date, only ten elasmosaur specimens have been collected from the Smoky Hill chalk, all of them incomplete. Only one included a skull. Luckily it was well preserved, with associated neck vertebrae; the skull's 20-inch length suggested that the animal it came from must have been a good 30 feet long. Bones of a much larger elasmosaur came from a barnyard in Logan County, Kansas, where the rancher who first found them thought they were "elephant bones" and didn't try to preserve them. From the size of the three vertebrae that were rescued at that site, it is apparent that the full animal would have measured 40 to 45 feet in length.

The body shape of the elasmosaurs was similar to that of the shorter-necked plesiosaurs in every way except the neck. *Elasmosaurus*, the elasmosaur species with the longest known neck, had more than 70 cervical vertebrae—10 times the number in the neck of a human or a giraffe. Most other elasmosaurs had 60 to 65 cervical vertebrae, and their necks represented more than half of their overall body length. Having such a long neck obviously posed some challenges in the daily life of these animals, but they still survived for millions of years. Our lack of understanding of those adaptations and challenges, however, has produced a number of serious misconceptions about how these animals lived.

The earliest drawings of long-necked plesiosaurs showed these sea monsters swimming on or near the surface. Some even had them resting on land, with their heads held up high on curving necks as if they were giant swans. Even the great American paleontologist E. D. Cope commissioned several drawings of plesiosaurs in this pose for his publications, matching his description of "tall, twining forms rising to the height of the masts of a fishing fleet, or like snakes twisting and knotting themselves together."

More recent studies of the vertebrae of the long-necked plesiosaur indicate that these animals could move their necks very little, neither up and down nor from side to side. Elasmosaurs appear not to have had the muscles necessary to lift a 20-foot-long neck weighing a ton or more. Likewise it is physically impossible for an animal floating under—not on—the water's surface to lift up such a long, heavy portion of its anatomy out of the water. Instead, we now believe that elasmosaurs held their necks straight out in front of them while swimming. Sideways movements of head and neck would have had the same effect as a rudder, turning the body in the same direction. By the same token, it would have been nearly impossible for an elasmosaur to swim in a straight line while swinging its head from side to side.

WEBLINK

Discover more about elasmosaurs at the official Sea Monsters website.

The skulls of all the plesiosaurs, including the long-necked ELASMOSAURS ▶, have eyes on top, suggesting that these animals generally looked either forward or up— another piece of evidence disproving the image of a swan-necked monster. Even if these animals could lift their heads far above the water, they would have had to rotate their skulls nearly 180 degrees in order for their eyes to peer back down at the surface of the water in search of prey. Such evidence all adds up to the conclusion that elasmosaurs raised their heads only as far out of the water as necessary in order to breathe. In fact, they probably spent most of their time fully submerged, head, neck, and all.

Creatures with eyes that faced upward probably approached their prey from below. Imagine this scenario: Spotting a school of fish, an elasmosaur moved toward it, swimming at a depth of 20 feet or so, deep enough that its body stayed hidden in the dimly lit water. Since the targeted fish would be busy looking around and above them for their own prey, the predator could approach unnoticed. It angled its neck upward by tilting its body, and only its small head ascended in among the targeted school of fish, thus never creating the same level of alarm of a huge predatory body. With quick side-to-side movements of its head, the elasmosaur could grab unwary fish, feeding on some without scaring off others.

This scenario, of course, is an imaginative reconstruction. We do not know exactly how elasmosaurs acquired their prey, but the scenario proposed would help explain the evolutionary advantage of such an extremely long neck. Or, perhaps, the long neck was an advantage for animals that floated at the surface in relatively shallow water, feeding on small invertebrates or other prey just below them on the ocean bottom.

Re-created for the film, juvenile elasmosaur "fossils" are found in an area that used to be covered by shallow waters, supporting the idea that their lives began in this kind of environment.

Fish try to escape the toothy jaws of a Styxosaurus *as it attempts to snatch a mouthful of fish. Elasmosaurs may have used stealth to stalk their prey.*

Since about 1895, only three elasmosaur specimens have been collected from the chalk of western Kansas, two by George Sternberg. In 1925, Sternberg collected a specimen consisting only of a left front limb that showed graphic evidence of its having been bitten by a large shark. A nearly complete specimen of another elasmosaur species was recently discovered in the Pierre shale of western Kansas, providing the best picture we have of the *Styxosaurus,* an elasmosaur that grew to more than 30 feet with a short tail and a long, slender neck that equaled its body in length. But few such fossils have been found. In fact, elasmosaur remains are rarely found in the western Kansas rocks, which preserve the record of the open ocean during the Late Cretaceous. Because of this absence, paleontologists have reasoned that these long-necked plesiosaurs preferred the safety of shallower waters near shore, where they were less likely to become the victims of large sharks or other predators.

Despite their inordinately long necks, the elasmosaurs' skulls were relatively small, measuring only 2 feet long, or about 5 percent of their total body length, even in

Elasmosaurs couldn't arch their long, one-ton necks high above the water: They were too heavy. Holding so much weight out of the water would have caused their lower bodies to raise up and tip forward. Nothing would stay out of the water for long.

the largest known species. The bones of elasmosaur skulls are tightly fused together, meaning that the jaw did not unhinge to engulf its prey, so we can get some idea of the size of the prey that these animals swallowed by measuring the distance between the jaws. All indications suggest that elasmosaurs swallowed their prey whole. Their long, sharply pointed, interlocking teeth more likely trapped prey rather than tore it into smaller pieces. So the diet of even the largest elasmosaurs was limited to fairly small prey like fish or squid. The remains of a large elasmosaur in western Kansas have revealed stomach contents of fish no bigger than 15 inches in length.

Once swallowed, the prey had to travel down the very long neck of the elasmosaur to the digestive tract. Plesiosaur remains often include a pile of rounded stones called gastroliths near the animal's midriff. Gastroliths, or stomach stones, are similar to bits of gravel or sand found in the gizzards of modern-day chickens and are an aid to digesting food that has been swallowed whole. Ranging from the size of a grapefruit to a grain of sand, they look like smooth rocks, ground together in the

process of macerating the prey, worn down, and polished. Plesiosaur gastroliths are often located in a relatively small area inside the ribs, suggesting that they might have been contained within an organ similar to a gizzard. Rolled around by muscular contractions of this portion of the digestive system, the gastroliths could have mashed up whole prey into a more digestible paste. One *Styxosaurus* specimen contained fish remains partway reduced to tiny bone fragments and short strings of vertebrae.

Sometimes the rock types can be identified as coming from a particular locality—a clue to the travels taken by these sea monsters through the Western Interior Sea. Gastrolith specimens have been found hundreds of miles from where that type of rock originated, suggesting that these elasmosaurs swam, and perhaps migrated annually, hundreds of miles.

An early theory proposed that gastroliths served another function for these huge marine reptiles. A heavy weight in the middle of the body of a swimming animal, their mass might have worked as ballast, keeping plesiosaurs at a comfortable depth in the water. While some have advanced this theory, the physical evidence may suggest otherwise. Usually less than ten pounds of gastrolith material have been found near a single animal, and the relation of that small amount of weight to the several-ton weight of an elasmosaur throws the ballast theory into question.

Like the short-necked plesiosaurs, elasmosaurs propelled themselves through the water by using their large, flattened limbs as wings to generate lift. Because of their

Research has shown that the structure of an elasmosaur's neck vertebrae did not permit the kind of bent, arched position seen in this 1996 rendering.

unusual body shape, elasmosaurs probably swam fairly slowly. Imagine trying to drive your car while sitting on a boom hanging 20 feet ahead of the engine. This was the physical challenge facing elasmosaurs continuously, and they were moving in three dimensions instead of two.

Swimming so slowly, elasmosaurs were probably easy targets for large sharks. Perhaps that explains why all of the elasmosaur specimens discovered so far in the Smoky Hill chalk are incomplete, appearing to be torn apart before the animal remains even reached the sea bottom. One specimen, a nearly complete paddle, shows deep bite marks across the upper limb bone. An approaching shark tried to snag a bite of elasmosaur paddle; instead it ripped the entire limb off at the shoulder joint and then abandoned it for some reason. In one remarkable find, George F. Sternberg found the bones of another elasmosaur in association with "hundreds of shark teeth."

Due to their size, shape, and speed, they could not chase down fast fish the way their short-necked cousins could. Nevertheless, they probably were graceful and deliberate in their movements, capturing their prey with quick head swipes while their bodies were suspended below, almost motionless in the water.

THE OCEAN'S TOP PREDATOR

In the film *Sea Monsters*, danger lurks in deep water as the dollies enter the territory of one of the deadliest hunters ever to live in the ocean: the *Tylosaurus*. Devouring everything it could swallow, the *Tylosaurus* sat atop the food chain with few serious threats to its dominance. The *Tylosaurus* belonged to the latest—and most successful—group of the reptiles to return to the sea during the Mesozoic period: the mosasaurs.

The mosasaurs' success may have been due to their unusual mix of characteristics, their style of swimming and hunting, or possibly the lack of serious competition in the waters by the time they gained dominance. By then, 95 to 90 million years ago, the ichthyosaurs had become extinct, and the big-headed pliosaurs were nearing extinction, possibly due to increased competition with faster, larger, and more advanced fish species such as *Xiphactinus* and the giant Ginsu sharks. In the Late Cretaceous seas, there was little competition present from other sea monsters to prevent the rise of mosasaurs.

SCALES OR SMOOTH?

Some mosasaur remains suggest they had scales and not smooth skin. One 1877 find included impressions of scales so clear that they could be counted: 90 to the inch. Other finds suggest that mosasaur skin changed over time and became smoother over the millennia.

The 5-foot-long skull belongs to a massive Tylosaurus proriger, nick-named "Sophie," who was collected in Texas in 2004.

A Tylosaurus proriger
*makes a meal out of an
unsuspecting shark. The
largest mosasaur in the
Western Interior Sea, it ate
just about anything: fish,
plesiosaurs, birds, and even
other, smaller mosasaurs.*

Found in Wadi Hitan, Egypt, these remains are a Basilosaurus, *a whale that lived about 40 million years ago when a sea called the Tethys covered much of northern Egypt.*

WHAT ABOUT THE MONSTERS swimming in the seas today? While most whales may have gentle reputations, sizewise they hold their own against sea monsters. Various species of modern whales grow as big or bigger than the plesiosaurs or mosasaurs found in the Late Cretaceous. Although more recently developed life-forms, their evolutionary journey has paralleled that of the ancient sea monsters. About 50 million years ago, during the Eocene epoch, land-dwelling mammalian ancestors returned to the sea. Recent paleontological discoveries have revealed that whale ancestors were artiodactyls, a group of animals that includes sheep, cows, pigs, camels, deer, and hippos. Fossils found in Pakistan in 2001 suggest an animal with a whale-like skull and sheep-like ankles. Paleontologists envision a creature called *Rodhocetus*, with the body like a sea lion and a head like a tylosaur. It would have had webbed feet on short, articulated limbs. While it would not have been able to travel long distances on land, it would have moved easily in the water.

◄ *Basilosaurus*, a primitive whale, grew to 60 feet long and thrived during the Late Eocene period, 39 to 34 million years ago. Tiny hind legs show its evolutionary origins as a land dweller. As these creatures evolved into the whales of today, those limbs dwindled into tiny splint-like bones.

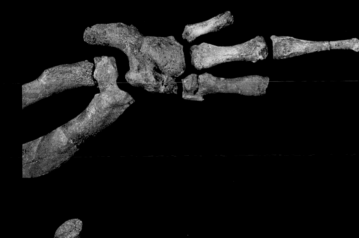

◄ Different kinds of teeth are clearly visible in this *Basilosaurus* jaw. Predominant in the fossil record of the southeastern United States, *Basilosaurus* is the state fossil of Alabama. Remains of this creature, whose name literally means "king lizard," have also been found in Eocene era rocks in Australia and Egypt.

◄ While they may not have been weight-bearing limbs, the ankle, foot, and toes of *Basilosaurus* were constructed and articulated much like those of a creature who walked on land. These fossils were excavated in 1990 at a site in Wadi Hitan, Egypt.

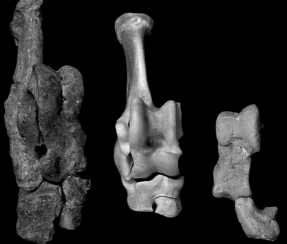

◄ Details in the configuration of fossilized ankle bones from prehistoric whales—*Rodhocetus*, left, and *Artiocetus*, right—suggest that these early whales shared a common ancestry with artiodactyls, or hoofed animals, such as the pronghorn antelope, whose ankle bone is shown here, center.

From the many different kinds of mosasaurs found in the fossil record, it is likely that several groups of ancestral mosasaurs entered the oceans at various places around the world at about the same time. The continents were closer together and sea levels were higher during the Late Cretaceous period than they are today, creating large, shallow seas over parts of North America, Europe, and Africa, through which the mosasaurs appear to have traveled. They appear to have spread rapidly around the world, migrating via shallower coastal waters. Similar species have been discovered as far apart as North America, Japan, and New Zealand.

About 95 million years ago, three different kinds of mosasaur lived in the Western Interior Sea: *Tylosaurus, Platecarpus,* and *Clidastes. Tylosaurus* was the largest, reaching about 30 to 40 feet in length. *Platecarpus,* 24 feet long, was likely the most common. *Clidastes,* the smallest and probably the most primitive of the group, measured about 15 feet in length. Within the space of a few million years, some mosasaur species evolved into truly huge sea monsters, some stretching to more than 50 feet. These giant mosasaurs became the apex predators in Earth's oceans during this time.

As best we can tell from the fossil record, the earliest mosasaurs were probably related to small semi-aquatic lizards called aigialosaurs that lived along ocean shores around the world from the late Jurassic through the Cretaceous periods. Much like modern marine iguanas, they may have fed in shallow waters but returned to land to breed. Unlike iguanas, though, mosasaur ancestors appear to have given live birth on land, since embryos have been found in aigialosaur remains. Once mosasaurs had fully adapted to live in the water, they still continued to bear live young.

Early investigators argued against live birth in mosasaurs, but remains have been discovered showing a mother mosasaur with babies in her abdomen. Baby mosasaurs seem to have measured between one and two meters at birth—a size that might make them vulnerable for large sharks, giant predatory fish, and other species of mosasaurs. Apparently more than enough mosasaur individuals reached reproductive age to

Fossilized mosasaur jaws suggest that these hunters used their cone-shaped teeth to grip but not to shred. Their doubly hinged jaws allowed them to swallow their prey whole.

maintain population growth over a long span of time. Paleontologists have noted the presence of many young mosasaurs in the Smoky Hill chalk , an area hundreds of miles from the nearest coast in the days of the Western Interior Sea, suggesting that mosasaurs gave birth in mid-ocean.

In overall appearance, mosasaurs resembled a modern crocodile but had paddles instead of legs and feet. Like the plesiosaurs, mosasaurs evolved to the point that their limbs could no longer support the weight of their large bodies out of water. While they may have been able to slither through shallow water like snakes, they would have been nearly helpless on dry land. Once beached, they would have died by suffocation or overheating. It appears that most mosasaurs used these paddles to steer their bodies while swimming. Early on in their evolution, mosasaur limbs ended in widely spread digits loosely joined by webbing to form a flexible paddle. Later forms evolved a tightly arranged and stiffer wing-like structure that may have been useful for hunting in shallow water or seaweed-rich environments.

The long, slender body of most mosasaurs was topped by a long, conical, narrow head. An expanded chest region suggests that, unlike snakes, mosasaurs still had the two lungs that their terrestrial ancestors had. A muscular tail, flattened vertically, propelled the animal through the water with a sinuous, snake-like movement. While modern sea snakes swim by undulating their entire body, mosasaurs swam mostly by using their tails. Their body vertebrae seem to have been relatively inflexible, so the body stayed stiff while the muscular tail moved. Although certainly capable of swimming long distances and remaining at sea indefinitely, mosasaurs probably could not keep up with the speedy short-necked plesiosaurs. What was lacking in speed was made up for in stealth. Mosasaurs were the consummate ambush predators, using rapid bursts of acceleration to overtake and capture their prey.

TYLOSAURUS PRORIGER
Order: *Squamata*
Cretaceous Period • North America
40 feet

BETWEEN 1870 AND 1880,
about 2,000 mosasaur specimens
were collected in Kansas alone,
together with fossils of giant fish,
pterasaurs, birds with teeth,
and even a dinosaur that had died
and floated out to sea.

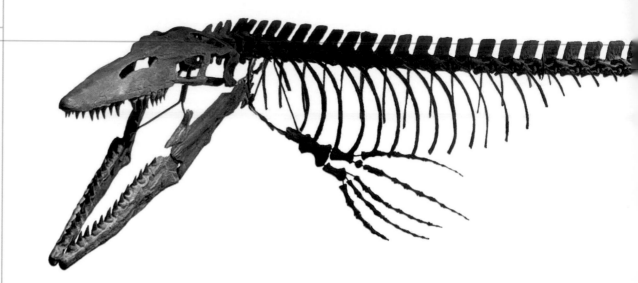

Most mosasaur teeth are cone-shaped without sharp cutting edges. Short of dismembering its prey by the sheer force of its bite, a mosasaur must have swallowed its catch whole and used its teeth to seize and grip. The jaw configuration of these sea monsters evolved to allow that possibility. The mosasaur's skull was flexible enough that it could open its mouth wide, engulf, and swallow large prey. A hinge (or quadrate) attaching its lower jaw provided additional fore and aft movement, while another flexible joint in the middle of each lower jaw opened outward as the prey was sucked into the mouth. As the lower jaw disengaged and moved forward, two extra rows of teeth on the roof of the mosasaur's mouth kept prey from escaping.

Although their primary diet appears to have been fish, mosasaurs ate just about anything that they could swallow. The preserved stomach contents of one large specimen of a tylosaur contained the bones of a smaller mosasaur, a *Hesperornis*, a fish, and possibly a shark. Charles H. Sternberg made the remarkable discovery of a 29-foot-long *Tylosaurus* that contained the remains of a juvenile plesiosaur inside its ribs. Numerous ammonite shells have been collected with what appear to be mosasaur bite marks, but there is some question as to whether they were caused by mosasaur teeth or small invertebrates called limpets attaching to the shells.

Mosasaurs probably preferred the shallower coastal waters, where prey was abundant. They excelled at open-water swimming, too, though, traveling through large bodies of water, as evidenced by the numerous fossils collected in Kansas from deposits in the middle of the Western Interior Sea, hundreds of miles from what would once have been the nearest land. From the number of remains discovered in these formations, it seems apparent that mosasaurs were living for long periods in mid-ocean during this period.

Life in the oceans of the Cretaceous was dangerous for all creatures, including mosasaurs. Evidence from the Smoky Hill chalk , including sharks' teeth embedded

Measuring over 40
feet long, the "Bunker
Tylosaur," discovered in
1911 by C. D. Bunker,
is the largest mosasaur find
in North America to date.

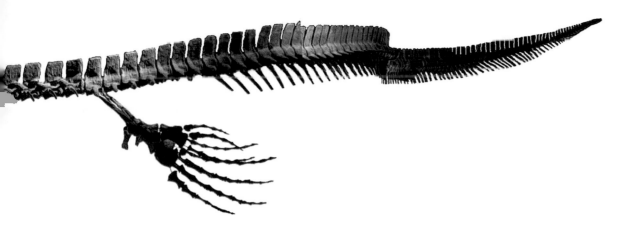

in partially digested mosasaur bones, indicates that large Ginsu sharks fed on mosasaurs. Perhaps they attacked live mosasaurs or scavenged on dead carcasses. More than likely, behaving like great white sharks of today, the Ginsu sharks attacked vulnerable mosasaurs—small, injured, or sickly—and never passed up a free meal on a dead mosasaur, either. The fossil record indicates, however, that during the time that mosasaurs were becoming bigger and more widespread, the Ginsu shark was becoming extinct. Did mosasaurs cause the extinction of these large sharks? No one knows for sure, but it seems reasonable that juvenile sharks were on the menu for hungry mosasaurs. With the success of mosasaurs, a population explosion occurred in the waters of the Late Cretaceous, creating pressure to expand into new territories. Although the origin, timing, and direction of these mosasaur migrations are not

Re-created for the film, this fossilized mosasaur jaw features deep indentations that appear to be bite marks caused by large Ginsu sharks.

known, new discoveries continue to reveal the extent to which they dispersed across the oceans of Earth.

As the age of dinosaurs ended, mosasaurs ruled supreme in Earth's oceans. They were beginning to invade freshwater environments such as estuaries, swamps, and rivers. And then they, and other sea monsters, disappeared. Paleontologists are exploring if they died off suddenly or if their extinction was gradual. Continued investigation of the fossil record might help uncover the ultimate fate of these sea monsters.

GLASSES ON

Rows of sharp, cone-shaped teeth line the gaping jaws of the Tylosaurus. *These teeth were used to grip and hold prey before swallowing it whole.*

THE UNDISPUTED TOP PREDATOR OF THE LATE CRETACEOUS was the *Tylosaurus*, a mosasaur that could grow up to 40 feet in length. Large, powerful swimmers, these voracious eaters hunted a wide variety of animals, from aquatic birds like the *Hesperornis*, above, to other sea monsters. Strong competition came from other tylosaurs; a heated confrontation between two tylosaurs, opposite, could be deadly.

Not even sharks were off limits to the Tylosaurus, which used its size and strength to its advantage to overcome this shark and devour it.

GLASSES OFF
FOR NEXT PAGE

CHAPTER FOUR

WHERE DID?
THEY GO?

Broad wings carry Pteranodons *over the Western Interior Sea. Pterosaurs became extinct about 65 million years ago.*

VER MILLIONS OF YEARS, THE WESTERN INTERIOR Sea teemed with these marine reptiles and their contemporaries, from microscopic plankton to gigantic tylosaurs, from the hard-shelled ammonites to the lumbering marine turtles. Dollies and elasmosaurs populated the shallows and ventured out on travels through the deeper waters. But today, none of these sea monsters swim the oceans. What could have happened to these prehistoric rulers of the deep?

All that time, geological change was rumbling beneath the seabed. Two tectonic plates along the western edge of North America were inching toward one another, one sliding under the other. Their slow collision pushed an enormous ridge of rock upward—part of this ridge would become the Rocky Mountains. Land that once laid hundreds, even thousands, of feet underwater lifted up into the open air. Volcanic eruptions caused by the collision of these tectonic plates

ENCHODUS
Order: *Salmoniformes*
Cretaceous Period • North America
4 feet

LEFT: *A dense school of* Enchodus *reflects the moonlight. Despite its large fangs, this fish was a popular meal for many predators in the Late Cretaceous.*

MODERN SEA MONSTERS APPEAR

The oceans today are still populated by sea monsters: giant mammals and sharks.

GALEOCERDO CUVIERI
Common Name: Tiger Shark
Evolved ca 48 M.Y.A.
18 feet long
A true omnivore, it has been known to eat just about anything: from fish, aquatic birds, and carrion, to human trash.

RHINCODON TYPUS
Common Name: Whale Shark
Evolved ca 33 M.Y.A.
40 feet long
The largest fish living on Earth, this massive shark eats mostly plankton and small crustaceans.

CETORHINUS MAXIMUS
Common Name: Basking Shark
Evolved ca 29–35 M.Y.A.
26 feet long
A filter feeder, this harmless shark is commonly seen swimming with its mouth wide open.

25 million years ago

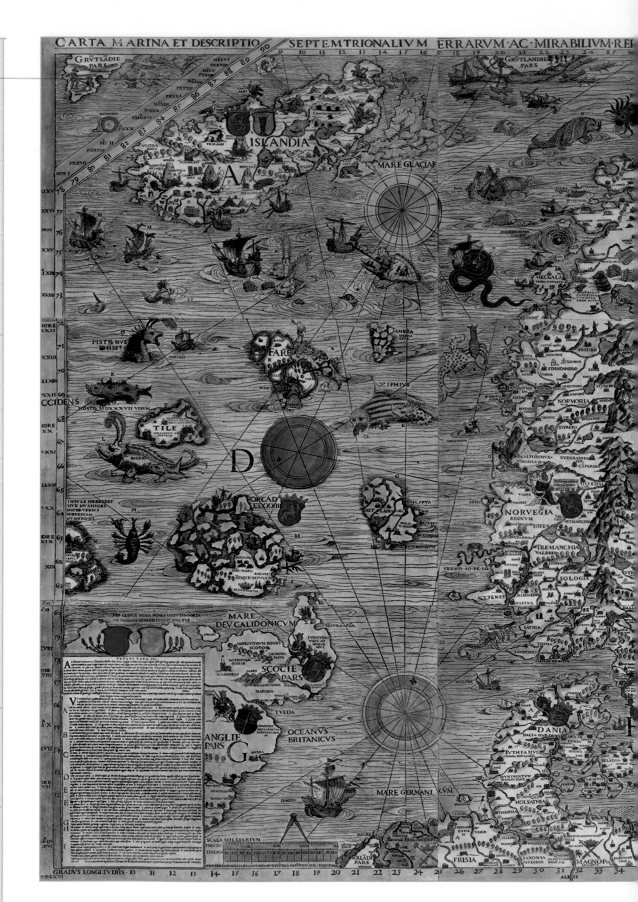

Sea monsters populate the far reaches of this 1549 Scandinavian map,

the Carta Marina. Were they fantasies or more modern "monsters"?

20

PHYSETER CATODON
Common Name: Sperm Whale
Evolved ca 20 M.Y.A.
60 feet long
Largest of the toothed whales,
they can swim at 20 knots.
They feed on giant squid.

15

CARCHARODON CARCHARIAS
Common Name:
Great White Shark
Evolved ca 11 M.Y.A.
20 feet long
The great white's scary reputa-
tion is well-deserved; it's the
world's largest predatory fish.

10

BALAENOPTERA MUSCULUS
Common Name: Blue Whale
Evolved ca 5–10 M.Y.A.
110 feet long
A gentle giant, the blue whale
is believed to be the largest
animal ever to live on Earth.

5

ORCINUS ORCA
Common Name: Killer Whale
Evolved ca 2–5 M.Y.A.
26 feet Long
A successful predator,
the killer whale is the largest
species in the dolphin family.

1

Present Day

spewed massive amounts of ash into the air. The Interior Sea began to dry up, revealing dry land where there was once water. Slowly North America began to take shape, establishing the continental outline and the landscape of plains and mountains that we now know.

These changes, which characterized the last 20 million years of the Cretaceous period, from about 85 to 65 million years ago, meant changing pressures on Earth's sea monsters. As ocean area shrank, territory was taken from them. This environmental change had an impact on the nature and number of microscopic plant and animal life in those waters. Those changes worked their way up the food chain, and creatures whose diets depended on certain species endangered by the climate change found their own lives in danger.

These changes would have occurred over hundreds of thousands of years. As centuries passed, hungry predators had to satisfy themselves with smaller catches. Eventually, even the most abundant and successful creatures, like the plesiosaurs and the mosasaurs, would begin to dwindle in numbers. Somewhere, one by one, the last of these prehistoric sea monster species died, disappearing from the face of the Earth but leaving their remains in the fossil record, to be discovered millions of years in the future.

EXTINCTION THEORIES

The scene above describes one theory of how Earth's sea monsters, the predominant ocean animals of the Late Cretaceous period, met with their extinction. According to this theory it happened slowly, over millions of years. Another theory blames one or more cataclysmic events, such as a meteor strike, and hypothesizes rapid, devastating consequences for all life on Earth. The two theories need not be mutually exclusive; perhaps the slow changes were already under way when a meteor struck Earth and sped up the extinction process.

However it happened, the fossil record does suggest a major change in the forms of life on Earth about 65 million years ago.

Geologists and paleontologists mark this momentous transformation as the shift from the Mesozoic to the Paleozoic era in geologic time, and they call it the "KT Boundary"—the boundary between the Cretaceous period, last of the Mesozoic era, and the Tertiary period, the first part of the Cenozoic era.

It is important to note that the extinction of species is a natural process. It occurs when species fail to adapt to changing conditions. More than 99 percent of all species that have ever lived on this planet are now extinct. The fossil record generally shows that vertebrate species exist for about 5 million years before they either evolve into one or more other species—or become extinct.

In addition to this normal cycle of species evolution and extinction, the fossil record suggests several dramatic extinction events on this planet. The first occurred about 450 million years ago. The biggest of all apparently occurred some 250 million years ago, when nearly half of all existing marine species died. Life recovered and flourished, only to face another major extinction about 200 million years ago and a smaller event at the end of the Jurassic period, about 150 million years ago, when most of the ichthyosaurs disappeared.

The major extinction event familiar to many people is the one that occurred some 65 million years ago at the KT Boundary. A huge number of species on Earth, we believe, became extinct all at about the same time. The list of animals that disappeared includes

Clouds of ash fill the sky after spewing from volcanoes of the Late Cretaceous period, covering the landscape of the North American west.

WEBLINK

Discover more about
extinction events at the
official Sea Monsters website.

all of the remaining dinosaurs, the pteranodons, the plesiosaurs, the mosasaurs, and many other species. The ◄ EXTINCTION was so sweeping and broad, it is understandable that theorists might search for a single monumental event to explain it.

So if such a cataclysmic event occurred, what exactly happened? Geological evidence now suggests that about 65 million years ago, an asteroid six miles wide—about the size of Mount Everest—crashed into Earth on the eastern edge of Mexico's Yucatan Peninsula, near the present-day town of Chicxulub. Such a collision must have been colossal, more devastating than anything the human mind can grasp. Its instantaneous effects would have spread out hundreds or thousands of miles, and its aftereffects would have spanned the entire globe. Much of the meteor itself must have vaporized, along with hundreds of cubic miles of rock near the impact site, creating a crater more than one hundred miles across and several miles deep. Geologists believe that they have found the massive crater caused by such a meteor, hidden under water

Under the Indian subcontinent exist huge pockets of basalt called the Deccan traps. These deposits date to roughly 68 to 60 million years ago. Some scientists postulate that volcanic eruptions at the KT boundary may have contributed to the mass extinction of dinosaurs and marine reptiles.

and sediment for millions of years but detectable today in many of the geologic features of eastern Mexico.

Judging from the shape of the crater remnants discovered in the Yucatan, researchers believe that the asteroid was traveling northwest when it entered Earth's atmosphere. If so, the force of its blast and aftereffects would have been especially strong toward the northwest—in other words, in the southern portion of the Western Interior Sea. The heat and blast effects would kill all life within hundreds of miles and send earth-quaking shocks, fires, and tsunami-scale waves even farther. Creatures living in those waters would have been decimated, hit by a blast more tremendous than any humanly engineered bomb. Large pieces of debris would fly out into the atmosphere so fast and high that they would reach low Earth orbit and then rain back down around the globe for weeks or months. Smaller dust particles would infuse the upper atmosphere, remaining there indefinitely, shutting off sunlight, cooling the planet, and creating the

A Tylosaurus arcs above the waves, its future uncertain, in this artist's interpretation of a cataclysmic Late Cretaceous meteor strike.

DEEP UNDER THE YUCATAN PENINSULA lie the remains of a buried crater, more than a hundred miles across, formed when a meteorite impacted Earth 65 million years ago. For decades, oil-drilling excavations near the city of Progreso, Mexico, had been turning up geological anomalies within a roughly circular region along the coastline of the Yucatan. Some rocks found as deep as 3,000 feet had unusual characteristics. Physical and chemical tests showed that they had been formed

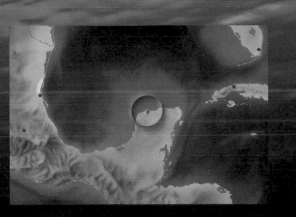

THE CHICXULUB CRATER:
Examination of the underlying geology of the circled area suggests that a massive asteroid or comet core struck near today's Chicxulub, Mexico, about 65 million years ago. The impact threw trillions of tons of dust into the atmosphere, affecting life and climate around the world.

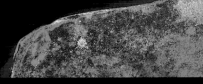

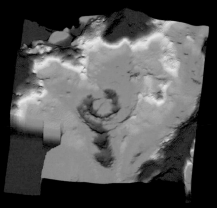

IMAGING THE IMPACT:
Global imaging technologies reveal the remains of what may have been the most extraordinary meteor strike in Earth's history. Shuttle radar topography (above) reveals an arc of underground troughs and cenotes, or groundwater springs. Landsat data (below) highlight the potential point of impact.

GRAVITY ANOMALY:
In the Chicxulub region, local gravitational fields vary significantly from the expected norms, Red indicates gravitational force higher than expected, blue lower than expected. Filled in with impact debris and sediment, the crater's center shows a negative gravity anomaly, distinctly different from surrounding rock.

IMPACT DEBRIS:
Around the world, in a geological stratum called the KT Boundary, rock specimens provide evidence of a cataclysmic event some 65 million years ago. This shocked quartz grain, its tiny fault lines caused by the impact, was blasted all the way from the Chicxulub site in Mexico to Haiti, where it was collected.

condition sometimes called a nuclear winter. Deprived of light, plant life would die off quickly. Animals that depended on a plant diet would starve to death in a short period of time. Soon larger, carnivorous animals would have nothing more to prey upon, and their kind would die off as well.

A METEORITE'S EFFECTS

To fully understand the effects such a meteorite collision might have, it is important to envision the state of Earth's environment at the time it seems to have occurred. Earth during the Cretaceous period had essentially been a water-world, with as much as 85 percent of the planet's surface covered by water. Oceans and shallow seas flooded the middle of North America, parts of Europe and Africa, the Middle East, and South America. These warm, shallow oceans had for millennia provided a favorable environment for many kinds of marine animals, from ammonites to sharks, from bony fish to flightless birds, and including a large variety of marine reptiles—our sea monsters. Many of the shallow seas around the continents were connected, especially in the Northern Hemisphere: a feature of the planet that still was enabling the mosasaurs to populate oceans around the world and essentially maintain their ascendancy as top predator in the oceans during the last few million years of the Cretaceous period.

Earth was warmer then than it is today. There were no polar ice caps; temperatures were cooler at the poles but still probably above freezing. The land near the poles could support lush forests, and dinosaurs roamed to the north and the south. Much of the land near the equator was arid or semi-arid, similar to that in present-day Mongolia. Deciduous trees and grasses had evolved by this time in Earth's history, and for the first time, these nutritious plants could support large herds of herbivorous dinosaurs and, indirectly, the large carnivorous dinosaurs that fed on them. The first birds began to take flight and were beginning to compete with the pterosaurs. Mammals were evolving, but as long as the dinosaurs were around, their species remained small.

Before the Chicxulub meteorite blasted into this world, it was a time when sea monsters were flourishing. Plesiosaurs like the dollies raised their young in the shallow water edges. In this world of sea monsters, the mosasaurs reigned supreme. Diversifying rapidly, their species had spread to every continent. Fast and ferocious, they may have driven at least one species of big shark into extinction. At the exact moment the meteorite struck, we do not know just how many of the sea monster species were alive, but we can conjecture what might have happened to them when the meteorite hit.

While size and bulk represented an evolutionary advantage to the plesiosaurs and mosasaurs in their watery environment, these characteristics did not save them from the blast. Many smaller species, such as the prehistoric ancestors of frogs and salamanders, appear to have been able to continue reproducing, their life cycles less affected by the cataclysmic event. Smaller species do tend to be more sensitive to environmental damage, so perhaps these ancestors were able to adapt more readily than the larger creatures.

Debris from the impact spewed into the air causing vast atmospheric changes. Changes in Earth's atmosphere might have damaged the population of underwater creatures, including those at the very bottom of the food chain, like microscopic plankton and the invertebrates. Those changes would move through the food chain, causing hunger and starvation from the bottom up.

PLATECARPUS

Order: Squamata

Cretaceous Period • North America

14 feet

These scenes of death and debilitation would, over the next hundreds or thousands of years, give way to new life on planet Earth. Slowly, in the wake of a cataclysmic event like the meteorite strike at Chicxulub, life must have begun to prosper once again. This time around, mammals became the dominant group of land animals, assuming the role that dinosaurs had played for millions of years before them. It was as if Mother Nature had been given a time-out and then resumed the evolution of life on this planet with a flourish.

But the age of the sea monsters was never to return to the planet. Where once the plesiosaurs and mosasaurs ruled supreme, new creatures now dominated. Some mammals took to the ocean, including one type of primitive whale, the *Basilosaurus,* that looked very much like a mosasaur. Other seagoing mammals would evolve, becoming larger than any walking on land. Never again, though, would marine reptiles grow to the size or numbers that they enjoyed during the Late Cretaceous.

TUSOTEUTHIS LONGA
(juvenile)
Reptilia: *Vampyromorphidia*
Cretaceous Period • North America
12 inches

A SLOWER THEORY

While the theory of a meteorite strike is exciting, it is perhaps more likely that sea monsters came to an end slowly, over hundreds of thousands of years. There are, in fact, some indications of a general collapse in the marine ecosystem at some point before the meteorite impact at Chicxulub. Many species of single-celled nannoplankton, including foraminifers, appear to have gone extinct within a short period of time. These organisms are responsible for converting the sun's energy into biological materials that can be utilized by other animals. Microscopic creatures like the nannoplankton represent the foundation for all of the productivity of the oceans. They also produce much of the oxygen that every animal needs to breathe.

When these microscopic organisms and the smaller consumers die en masse, it sends a ripple effect felt throughout the entire food web, from the bottom to the top. First invertebrates and the small fish that feed on the nannoplankton starve and die. The larger fish that depend upon smaller prey also starve and die off, and so it continues up the food chain. Mosasaurs, plesiosaurs, and other large marine predators at the very top of the ecosystem soon find themselves without adequate food supplies, and ultimately they starve to death, too. A slow scenario such as this, occurring over thousands of years, is not as spectacular as the image of an asteroid the size of Mount

LEFT: *The temperate climate in North America during the Late Cretaceous could support lush forests, herds of plant-eating duckbilled dinosaurs, and the predators that hunted them.*

ALBUM: UNCOVERING MONSTERS

Paleontologist Elizabeth Nicholls and colleague work on the massive skull of an excavated ichthyosaur in 1999.

THE MORE PALEONTOLOGISTS DIG, the more sea monsters they discover. Some embellish our understanding of the species already identified, while others are different enough to warrant new names and places on the marine reptiles' family tree. All that is known about ichthyosaurs increased immensely, for instance, after Canadian paleontologist Elizabeth Nicholls discovered massive fossilized remains along the Sikanni Chief River in British Columbia. It took six years and three difficult fieldwork seasons for Nicholls and her team to excavate the full-body fossil from the rocky streambed. The animal stretched nearly 70 feet from snout to tail. The skull alone weighed a ton and a half once. It was the largest ichthyosaur ever discovered. One new piece of information provided by Nicholls's discovery came from the absence of any teeth in the jaw of this huge specimen. Fossils of smaller, presumably younger ichthyosaurs did include teeth. Perhaps these creatures lost their teeth when they matured. If so, their diet must have changed simultaneously, from fish and larger creatures they gripped with their teeth to small invertebrates that they drew into their mouths by suction. The size of this creature's mouth (9 feet long and several feet wide) meant it could swallow just about anything it wanted. She and her colleagues agreed to called it *Shonisaurus sikanniensis,* after the river where they found it.

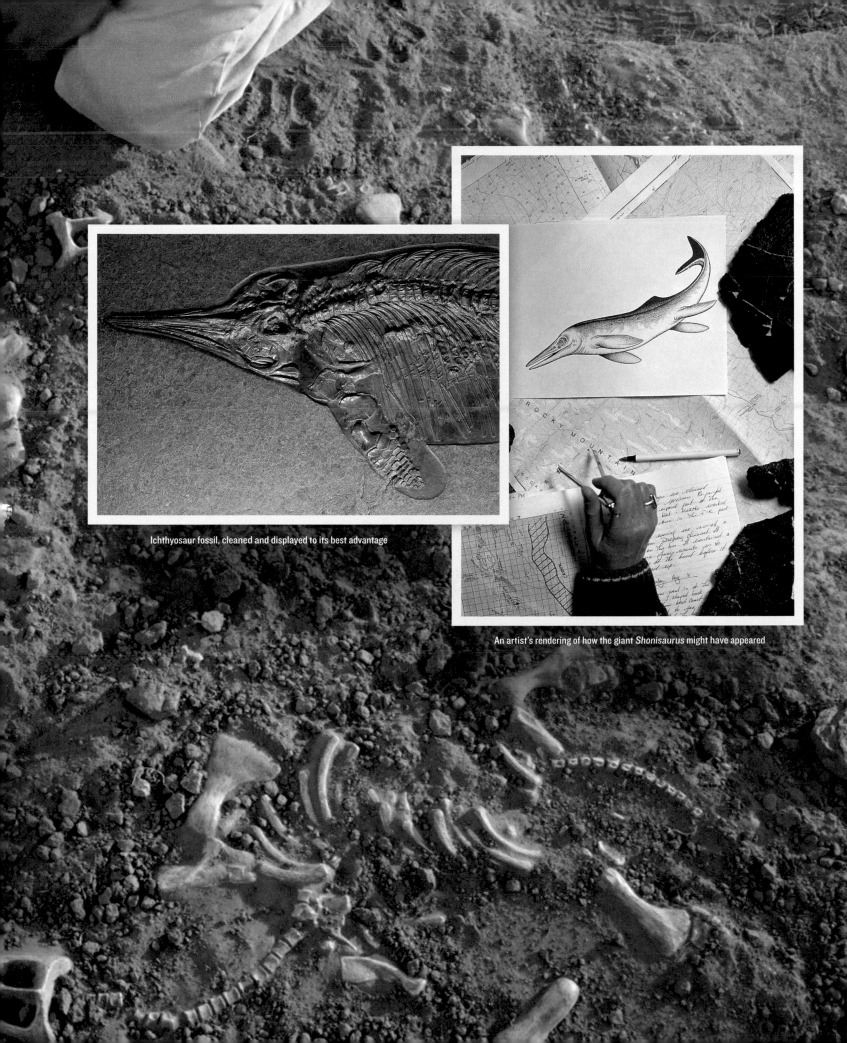

Ichthyosaur fossil, cleaned and displayed to its best advantage

An artist's rendering of how the giant *Shonisaurus* might have appeared

Fossilized vertebrae from a *Tylosaurus kansasensis*

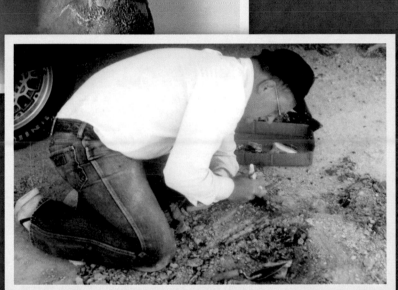
On a dig, the author excavates a new sea monster find.

Other new species of sea monsters have also been identified and named in the past decade, representing a proliferation in the kinds of sea monsters that thronged Earth's waters in prehistoric times. A new species of tylosaur, *Tylosaurus kansasensis,* was announced in 2005, named for the Indian tribe (Kaw or Kansa) for which the state of Kansas was also named. That same year, several new species of plesiosaur were publicly identified as well, based on specimens excavated in Canada and in Japan. A new type of mosasaur took on a name that marked its place of origin and the man who discovered it: *Dallasaurus turneri,* found near Dallas, Texas, by Van Turner. Turner, an amateur fossil finder, found a fossilized vertebra in the upturned earth of a construction site in 1989. He excavated associated remains as he could and took them to paleontologists at the Dallas Museum of Natural History and Southern Methodist University. Sixteen years later a scientific journal article announced the new species, considered one of the earliest species in the long evolutionary history of the mosasaurs. While *Dallasaurus* measured only three feet long, its descendants grew to become the giants of the Late Cretaceous oceans.

BACKGROUND: *In this scene from the film, a paleontologist works carefully and slowly to uncover a plesiosaur fossil.*

Everest hitting Earth. It's a slower story that ends with more of a whimper than a bang, but some experts feel that this explanation is the more plausible one for the extinction of the marine reptiles at the end of the age of sea monsters.

SURVIVORS

One type of marine reptile did survive, however, and its evolutionary ancestors live among us in the world today. Of the creatures that appear in the film *Sea Monsters*, marine turtles are the only apparent survivors of the great extinction that caused the disappearance of the sea monsters of the Late Cretaceous. While the giant marine turtle varieties, such as *Protostega gigas* and *Archelon*, did become extinct, some smaller varieties did not. Perhaps it was because marine turtles were egg-layers and were able to produce more young than the other marine reptiles. Perhaps it was because they were capable of feeding on things that survived as well, food sources different from those on which plesiosaurs and mosasaurs depended. We simply do not know why the marine turtles of the Late Cretaceous period survived and other sea monsters did not.

The relatively rare leatherback—the largest living turtle alive today—represents the closest descendant of any one of the giant marine turtles featured in the film. Reaching a body length up to nine feet and a weight of half a ton at maturity, these marine animals probably mirror their prehistoric ancestors in a number of ways. Their carapaces are not the hard outer shell of any other turtle, but instead are made of dense connective tissue stretched over a ribbed structure, a configuration reminiscent of the fossil remains of Late Cretaceous marine turtles found in the Smoky Hill chalk .

Leatherbacks can be found in the Atlantic, Pacific, and Indian Oceans. They are known to be able to dive nearly 5,000 feet. They feed primarily on jellyfish. Like their ancestors. female leatherbacks come ashore to lay eggs. Sixty-five days later the baby leatherbacks hatch and make their way straight into the sea. They are vulnerable to heat and predators in that early scramble. Those risks are not the greatest threat to the leatherback today, however. Mankind poses the greatest threat to these creatures. whose numbers have dropped precipitously in the last several decades. Marine scientists have requested a moratorium on harmful fishing practices to save the leatherback, this longtime evolutionary survivor, from extinction by human hands in the 21st century.

LEFT: *The hawksbill turtle, found in tropical waters, traces its ancestry to prehistoric marine turtles. An even closer modern descendant is the relatively rare leatherback turtle.*

Moving in for the kill, a Cretoxyrhina *shark bears down fast—its mouth wide open and jaws poised to srike. This shark was one of the top predators in the Western Interior Sea.*

Paleontologists believe that the Cretoxyrhina *probably used hunting techniques very similar to the modern great white shark.*

The bone-shearing teeth of the Cretoxyrhyna *shark gave it a "razor-sharp" nickname: the Ginsu shark. Today, shark teeth are among the most common fossil finds in Kansas.*

GLASSES OFF
FOR NEXT PAGE

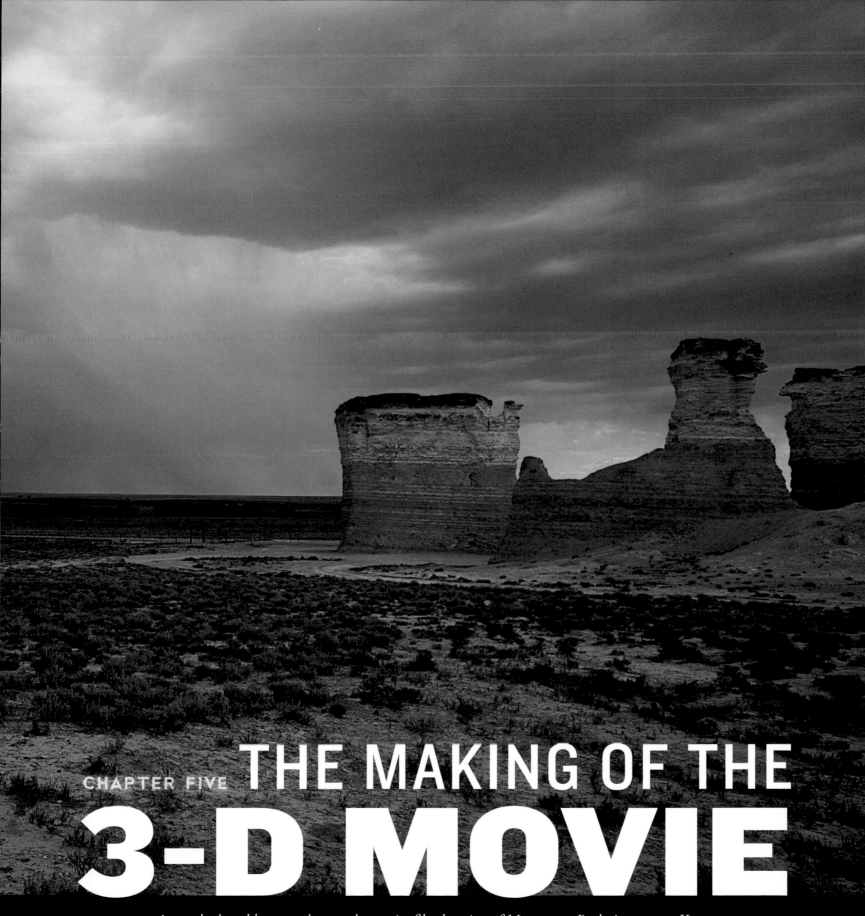

CHAPTER FIVE

THE MAKING OF THE
3-D MOVIE

A moody sky adds atmosphere to the on-site film location of Monument Rocks in western Kansas.

T HE DECEMBER 2005 NATIONAL GEOGRAPHIC MAGAZINE reached out and grabbed readers with as much bite as the prehistoric creature depicted on its cover. A *Dakosaurus andiensis,* a prehistoric crocodilian, surged up from the page with jaws full of sharp teeth. "Sea Monsters," the headline read. "Scientists bring 'Godzilla' back to life." Paleontologists had recently excavated an entire skull of a *Dakosaurus* in Patagonia, Argentina, in a landlocked site that was once part of the Pacific Ocean. "It is one of the most evolved members of the crocodilian family," said paleontologist Diego Pol, "and also one of the most bizarre." Working from that skull, scientists and artists collaborated to create the magazine's cover, a thrilling image that evoked with near-three-dimensional vitality a moment on Earth 135 million years ago. Inside the issue were more ancient sea monsters, like elasmosaurs and mosasaurs, that lived millions of years apart from each other.

LEFT: *Nicknamed Godzilla, a* Dakosaurus *defends its meal from a group of hungry pterosaurs. This image graced the cover of* NATIONAL GEOGRAPHIC *in December 2005.*

THE MAKING
OF THE MOVIE

A short list of movie making milestones, from start to finish.

The crew hoses off the waterproof housing that protects the heavy

3-D camera used to capture underwater footage in the Bahamas.

12/06

WHEN: December 2006
WHAT: Modeling of the animated creatures continues. Weekly meetings with experts are held to review the sea creatures for accuracy and realism.

01/07

02/07

WHEN: February 2007
WHAT: The first of the major character models are approved. As each characters' body shapes, colors, and textures are finalized, they will be composited into animated scenes.

03/07

04/07

05/07

WHEN: June 2007
WHAT: After undergoing dozens of revisions, the official script is finalized. Movie narration and soundtrack are recorded.

06/07

07/07

WHEN: July 2007
WHAT: Animation of all action sequences is complete, and work begins on the first projection print.

08/07

WHEN: October 2007
WHAT: The end-result of years of hard work and meticulous research: *Sea Monsters: A Prehistoric Adventure* premieres in movie theaters throughout the United States.

09/07

10/07

11/07

NOTHOSAURUS

DAKOSAURUS

ARCHELON

TEMNODONTOSAURUS

KRONOSAURUS

THALASSOMEDON

TYLOSAURUS

SHONISAURUS

Inside the magazine, equally vivid computer-generated images re-created the appearance and behavior of other marine reptiles, species that dominated Earth's oceans for hundreds of millions of years. While remains of such seagoing creatures were discovered well before those of dinosaurs, they had never become as familiar to the public as their terrestrial counterparts. Now the National Geographic Society had the opportunity, thanks to the confluence of new scientific discoveries and new graphic technologies, to bring these creatures into view as never before.

SEEING SEA MONSTERS

For the magazine article, a team of artists and consultants collaborated to create the amazing computer-generated imagery highlighted in the issue. Three-dimensional computer models were created for each marine reptile based on the fossil record. The first step was to look at the fossilized bones to create a three-dimensional skeleton. It's complicated work; skeletons are often incomplete, while the fossilization process can distort and even flatten bones. But using these fossils would be key in determining realistic movements for these creatures, making them hunt and swim in anatomically correct ways.

Using input from paleontologists, the artists began by generating computerized wireframe models for nine different creatures. Then the body was fleshed out with muscles and skin before textures and colors could be added. It was important to forget preconceived ideas of how a sea monster should look. The imagery needed to move closer to what the historic record suggests, not what science fiction has imagined. All these details poured into the imaginations of artists and computer programmers, who created an interactive display of sea monsters, their three-dimensional

appearances, and, in a couple of cases, their hunting habits, which were featured online as an interactive companion piece to the December 2005 "Sea Monsters" cover story.

The December 2005 cover story was just the beginning. These marine reptile depictions were engaging, highly informative, and would lead to something more. How about projecting these animals on a giant movie screen? How about making them 3-D? How about bringing them to life—or at least bringing them as close to life as one could do in the 21st century? How about showing the world in which they lived and the creatures who shared the seas with them? The idea of a 3-D big-screen movie about sea monsters intrigued everyone, and a film started to take shape.

FINDING THE STORY

From the beginning, it was important to pick a single time setting for the *Sea Monsters* story. The magazine could portray creatures from a broad array of periods—from the Triassic's *Nothasaurus* from 230 million years ago to the *Thalassomedon* from 95 million years ago in the Cretaceous, but this approach would be difficult to pull off on film. To tell a unified story, the movie had to be set in a single time and place, where all the creatures could interact with one another.

A remarkable fossil find helped the *Sea Monsters* team to select the late Cretaceous period, 82 million years ago. The inspiration came from a short note that paleontologist Charles Sternberg had written about a discovery of his in Kansas in 1918. It was an unusual find, a mosasaur with a small plesiosaur preserved inside. Sternberg had reported it at the Kansas Academy of Sciences meeting in 1918, but the proceedings from that meeting were not published until 1922. All they contained was a one-paragraph announcement, easy to overlook, and an indication that the specimen had been sent to the United States National Museum—today's Smithsonian Institution. The new mosasaur specimen was also described in a 1921 *Scientific American* article, but the interesting stomach contents were not mentioned. In short, Sternberg's discovery got lost in the scientific literature, until Mike Everhart, paleontologist (and

TEMNODONTOSAURUS PLATYDON

Reptilia: *Ichthyosauria*

Jurassic Period • Europe

30 feet

ABOVE: *A modern 18-wheeler would be overwhelmed in length by one of the giant ichthyosaurs that roamed Earth's oceans 100 million years ago.*

Cruising a lagoon in what is now Germany, the Henodus, *one of the marine reptiles called placodonts, was wider than it was long. Remains found in Europe date to 225 million years ago.*

later film consultant), brought it back into the light in 2001. As it turned out, this one-of-a-kind specimen became the centerpiece of the film *Sea Monsters*.

In the context of Everhart's research on mosasaurs, Sternberg's reported find was a very important specimen. Mosasaurs were known to have eaten many kinds of animals as prey, including other mosasaurs, but no one had ever found evidence of their eating plesiosaurs. In November 2001, Everhart visited the Smithsonian to look at the big mosasaur specimen that Sternberg had collected and, more importantly, to examine the plesiosaur that had been preserved inside as the mosasaur's last meal.

Everhart found both the mosasaur and the plesiosaur, although they had been curated separately. The mosasaur had been on permanent display in the Ancient Seas exhibit, but the juvenile plesiosaur bones had been in storage for nearly 80 years when Everhart first encountered them. Records verified their association, however. Everhart found a tag on the plesiosaur remains, written in Charles Sternberg's hand, reading "Half digested plesiosaur bones between the ribs of No. 17." "They were not much to look at," recalls Everhart, "but they were definitely from a young plesiosaur." Many bones were missing, probably reflecting remains carried away by sharks as they scavenged the carcass of the mosasaur. Part of the mosasaur's tail and limbs were missing, too, as Sternberg himself had noted. Although the collection of bones did

The inspiration for the film, this 30-foot-long tylosaur is displayed in the Smithsonian Museum of Natural History. It was discovered by George F. Sternberg and sent there.

not represent a "huge plesiosaur" as claimed by Sternberg, his remarkable discovery was verified and published in an article by Everhart in 2004.

This remarkable find placed the action for *Sea Monsters* squarely in the Late Cretaceous period, the time when both a mosasaur and plesiosaur would have coexisted. Their environment would be the Western Interior Sea that covered much of North America during that time. Their counterparts would be the other creatures who lived, swam, hunted, and died alongside them. Eventually a story line was concocted that pulled in more than 25 different species.

As time and place were chosen, a story began to take shape. It traced the journey of two juvenile plesiosaurs who travel from their safe birthplace in the shallows to the dangerous deeper waters of the open ocean, populated by fierce, hungry predators. On their way, the plesiosaur pair encounter the strange, mysterious, beautiful, and sometimes terrifying creatures of the Western Interior Sea. The story would even feature an encounter with a deadly mosasaur, bringing to life Charles Sternberg's unique discovery in the Kansas chalk.

But there were other important figures in the story besides the plesiosaur and mosasaur. From the first, the film's creators wanted to use real fossil discoveries to explain how we've come to understand these and other sea monsters and the world in which they lived. To do that, the story of fossil finders would need to be shown as well. Re-creations of the Sternberg digs and many others from Europe, the Middle East, Australia, and North America would need to be woven into the story. Each one demonstrates how the fossils found there built an understanding of how these creatures behaved and interacted. Scenes would flash forward to re-creations of fossil digs to show what scientists have learned about this 82-million-year-old world. Writers roughed out each plot and interwove them, one with another, into the complex back-and-forth that would ultimately show what the sea monsters' world looked like and how scientists came to understand it—all on the big screen.

CAPROBERYX

Order: *Beryciformes*

Cretaceous Period • North America

4 inches

CREATING FOSSIL FINDS

Filming the re-creations of the fossil digs took place where sea monster fossils had actually been discovered—the Smoky Hill chalk of western Kansas. Scouts came to Kansas long before the first camera arrived. Production teams visited a number of localities that had been suggested for each scene in the film. They had to scope out

Smooth sailing through realistic waters marks successful completion of the animated vision of Dolichorhynchops.

MANY MONTHS OF PAINSTAKING RESEARCH and development went into creating *Sea Monsters'* main character, a young female plesiosaur called *Dolichorhynchops*, called "dolly" in the film for short. At each stage, professional paleontologists collaborated with visual effects artists and computer animation specialists to create sketches and computer-generated models that rendered every detail of anatomy, movement, and behavior as realistically as possible. Once the shape, movements, and behaviors were approved, the dolly model was digitally integrated into a marine background. Imagery of other creatures known to have shared her environment were then brought into each scene. Every gesture, every move, and every companion creature in *Sea Monsters* had to be examined and approved by the film's scientific advisors, a painstaking yet necessary procedure in order to create an experience that is not only thrilling but also as scientifically accurate as possible in its representation of life on Earth and underwater 85 million years ago.

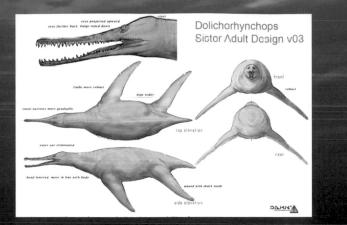

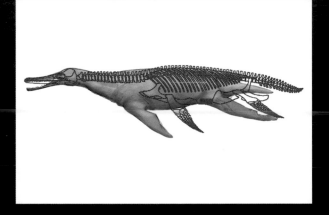

Female Dolly

Mother Dolly

◀ STEP ONE:

First, working from the fossil record and existing imagery, artists drafted sketches of dolly from all angles. Scientific advisors studied the sketches, calling for minute changes in the shape, relationship, and orientation of her anatomy. Sketches also helped artists and scientists communicate about the ways in which dolly could move—and couldn't.

◀ STEP TWO:

Computer-enhanced imagery let artists and paleontologists compare the fossil record with the illustrations under way. Here a computer-generated full skeleton of a *Dolichorhynchops* is overlaid on a working sketch of dolly. The comparison shows that the sketch needs revision, with her paddles repositioned farther back on her body.

◀ STEP THREE:

After two-dimensional drawings from all perspectives, a three-dimensional model was computer-generated. Drafting software can rotate the image, a necessary step toward illustrations destined for the 3-D screen. This base model became the prototype for all subsequent representations of dolly as her character moves through various episodes.

◀ STEP FOUR:

Next, artists applied color and texture. Paleontologists can only make educated guesses about such features of the sea monsters of the Late Cretaceous. For example, like many marine predators of today, the *Dolichorhynchops* might have found evolutionary benefits in the "counter shading" of a darker dorsal area and a lighter underbelly.

*Production designer
Charles Butcher readies
a reproduction fossil of a
Xiphactinus for filming
in the chalk near Wildcat
Canyon, Kansas.*

the lay of the land and secure permission to film from the landowners. Actors were cast to play the paleontologists, but their excavations needed to be created.

Where do you go to get a complete 30-foot-long skeleton of a mosasaur? How about a 13-foot-long giant fish with another fish inside? The answer is: Triebold Paleontology, a company specializing in museum-quality cast skeletons. Dave Ehlert and his staff were already familiar with the sea monsters of Kansas. Their Rocky Mountain Dinosaur Resource Center, a museum in Woodland Park, Colorado, includes a reproduction of the 45-foot-long Bunker tylosaur found in Kansas in 1911, the largest mosasaur fossil ever found in North America. "Ironically, Triebold Paleontology has specialized in making completely 3-D skeletons free of matrix and with compressive distortion of the fossils removed, while this project required that we place the casts back into the artificial rock and return them to their original compressed and distorted condition . . . a complete reversal of our usual technique, says Michael Triebold. Using solid urethane and urethane foam over wood and metal armatures, Triebold's team cast highly detailed reproductions of the very fossils that Charles Sternberg and his sons found in the chalk. Now the filming staff could go bury them in the dirt at the site of each scene, so they could be uncovered dramatically by the actors during their "excavations."

In the middle of June 2006, the film crew was on-site and filming in western Kansas. Film consultant Mike Everhart met them in western Gove County, where they were shooting Charles Sternberg's historic discovery of plesiosaur bones inside the remains of a giant mosasaur. The film shows Charles Sternberg and his two sons, George and Levi, digging out the mosasaur skeleton on the east side of a chalk formation called Monument Rocks. In the background can be seen a pickup truck; farther back, there is a campsite with a tent. BEHIND THE SCENES ▶, creating this historic moment, was a small army of production people and equipment, both behind the cameras and hidden behind the rocks in the background. Outside the camera frame sat trailers for costumes, makeup, and props, along with two fully-equipped canteen trucks that had driven in from California to feed the whole group while they were in the field.

During the filming process, Mike Everhart served as a technical advisor on paleontology for the director, the production staff, and the actors. While he helped them understand the science of what they were enacting—down to the detail of how to pronounce *Tylosaurus* and *Xiphactinus* convincingly—they poured their talents into the work of re-creating not only the fossil dig scenarios but also the personalities and mannerisms of famous paleontologists like the Sternbergs.

The process of creating and filming a scene is intense, in part because of the cost in time and money. Everyone involved takes it very seriously. When someone says, "Quiet on the set," all talking stops, and all eyes focus. Every shot takes time to set up, getting the actors in place and making sure nothing extraneous is moving in the background. One day the crew and actors worked through the afternoon at Monument Rocks, completing the scene just before sunset. One important shot remained to be filmed as the light faded. Charles Sternberg is sitting at his camp table, drawing what he thought the mosasaur would have looked like as he swallowed the smaller plesiosaur. The scene fades to a close-up of Sternberg's hand poised above his drawing, then makes a transition back into an animated segment. "In what is probably one of the smallest bit parts ever filmed for a movie," says Mike Everhart, "it was my hand that was filmed, several days later. How's that for movie trivia?"

WEBLINK

Discover more about the making of the film at the official Sea Monsters website.

Re-creating authentic paleontological excavations, screen actors sometimes used high-tech tools, sometimes simple pencil and paper.

CREATING AN UNDERWATER WORLD

Cameras rolled not only in Kansas but also in the Bahamas. The tropical waters and calcium carbonate platform there became a perfect, accurate-looking

Order: *Tselfatiiformes*
Cretaceous Period • North America
6 feet

backdrop to emulate that of the Western Interior Sea 82 million years ago. Using heavy 3-D cameras that were specially equipped with waterproof "housings," filmmakers took a variety of shots from above and below the water in order to reflect the variety of the sea monsters' environment, from the safe shallows to the deeper open water. These shots would serve as scenery for the animated action, which would be produced later.

Creating the animated marine reptiles and their contemporaries involved a team of scientific consultants. Joining Mike Everhart as advisors on the film were Ken Carpenter of the Denver Museum of Nature and Science and Glenn Storrs of the Cincinnati Museum Center. All three brought years of hands-on field experience and scholarly research to ensure that every little detail matched the scientific record.

As with the animals created for the December 2005 magazine issue, visual effects artists began by creating computer models for all the creatures in the film, from the main characters, like the tylosaurs, to

VISITING SEA MONSTERS

*To see sea monsters on display,
visit one of these exciting museums:*

STERNBERG MUSEUM
Hays, Kansas

FICK FOSSIL AND HISTORY MUSEUM
Oakley, Kansas

**UNIVERSITY OF KANSAS
MUSEUM OF NATURAL HISTORY**
Lawrence, Kansas

**UNIVERSITY OF NEBRASKA
STATE MUSEUM**
Lincoln, Nebraska

**ROCKY MOUNTAIN
DINOSAUR RESOURCE CENTER**
Woodland Park, Colorado

**DENVER MUSEUM
OF NATURE AND SCIENCE**
Denver, Colorado

the bit players, like the baculites. Design began with review of actual fossil skeletons, complemented by any works of paleoart that the science advisors considered reliable. For every one of the animals destined to play a part in the animation, computer graphics artists began by building reconstructions. Each was reviewed in fine detail by the team of science advisors. Iterations of these models went back and forth between the designers and scientists until finally the scholarly experts were satisfied that the model reflected current scholarship and knowledge currently held about that particular animal.

Once the base models were complete, artists had a foundation to work from, a sense of the overall shape of each marine reptile. Next came the lengthy task of adding color and texture to each animal, balancing aesthetics for the sake of the film with facts from the fossil record. Again, there were several rounds of communication between the artists and scientists, with comments and critiques, changes and revisions. Some of the creatures—like the *Pteranodon* and *Hesperornis*, the flightless marine bird— required months of design and redesign until experts were 100 percent satisfied.

*To represent the marine
environment of Earth in the Late
Cretaceous, the film production team
shot scenes above and below the
turquoise waters of Pelican Cay
National Park in the Bahamas.*

A Ginsu shark attacks a juvenile tylosaur in Dan Varner's 1999 painting.

AS SOON AS EARLY 19TH-CENTURY SCIENTISTS began publicizing their fossil finds, artists began sketching pictures, imagining how these never-to-be-seen creatures might have looked and behaved. The first such renderings were strictly anatomical, such as those drafted by the French scientist Baron Georges Cuvier himself. Cuvier carefully drew the bones that he and others studied, arranged as they might have been in a living animal, then gently added outlines to suggest an animal in the flesh.

Soon artists began painting landscapes and placed the creatures together in imagined environments. In the 1830s, George Scharf, an English painter, created some of the earliest depictions of prehistoric marine reptiles and their interactions in their world. One of Scharf's renderings shows a shallow body of water near land. Pterosaurs swoop high in the air, while the waters beneath are densely packed with sea creatures. Long-necked creatures swim with their heads and necks protruding (inaccurately) high above the water. Short-necked plesiosaurs have big round eyes and long, narrow snouts filled with teeth. They appear to be the dominant hunters in Scharf's depiction of the Jurassic period. When creating his figures, Scharf relied on information from newly discovered remains to calculate the size and proportion of the creatures.

In the 19th century, George Scharf imagined this underwater Jurassic scenario.

Doug Henderson created this modern depiction of elasmosaurs in the waves.

A Cretaceous crocodilian does battle in Raul Martin's illustration.

Self-taught artist Julius Csotonyi drew this *Ichthyosaurus communis*, a Jurassic sea monster.

The first three-dimensional prehistoric panorama was unveiled in Sydenham, England, in 1854. Working closely with a scientist, English artist Benjamin W. Hawkins built lifesize models of prehistoric creatures, including several of the sea monsters, out of iron and concrete. In all, 35 figures were erected in the park (which featured a six-acre lake), captured in life-like poses to help tourists picture a world many millennia old. Soon 3-D models like Hawkins's became standard fixtures in natural history museums, and a curious public came to know the extinct animals of prehistory as well as they knew those still alive in the far corners of their world.

Today, modern paleoimagery draws heavily on the latest scientific findings. Artists like Doug Henderson, Raul Martin, and Dan Varner rely on data from paleontologists and their digs. Using evidence from the fossil record, they create dynamic, vivid scenarios that show ancient reptiles and the worlds they inhabited. The artists who created the imagery for the film *Sea Monsters* were no different. Working closely with a team of expert consultants, the animation team created realistic paleoimagery for the movie, making sure each creature behaved the way the fossil records indicated.

ABOVE: *During the animation process, a team of experts made sure the depictions of all creatures, both the big and small, were in line with current science.*

TYLOSAUR MOVEMENT APPROACH I

When swimming swiftly, the paddles stay folded against the body

TYLOSAUR MOVEMENT APPROACH II

The powerful tail undulates from side to side.

TYLOSAUR MOVEMENT APPROACH III

The head and body remain stiff as the tylosaur swims over.

While one team of artists was working on texturing, another was working on animation. The question was, for each species of animal, just how did they move? Fossils may suggest the contours of a body shape, and occasionally they provide hints as to the covering of the body, but the still, silent record must be analyzed imaginatively to set these animals into motion. It's a question of anatomy and physics projected back millions of years.

Making these creatures move began with a look at modern creatures. Scientists suggested that the visual-effects artists use their movements to model locomotion. Take a look at the penguin to see how the paddle-like limbs of a *Dolichorhynochops* moved, they suggested. Study a crocodile as the model for movement of a nothosaur. For the primary characters of the film, entire swim cycles were developed to show, in an animated sketch, how the animal looked in motion from every direction. Getting the animations to show the correct movement of the paddles on the plesiosaurs was a particularly difficult problem between the paleontologists and the animators, in part because there is no modern animal with which to compare them. Early versions of the animation had the dollies and styxosaurs moving their paddles in ways that would have dislocated the limbs from the shoulder and hip joints of the living animal.

Once again, the creative process was a lengthy back-and-forth between creators and experts. Mosasaurs and plesiosaurs did not swim around with their mouths open, and they did not swing their head from side to side while swimming. Styxosaurs could not support their necks high out of the water. Those who knew the fossil record well would examine the movement created in an animation and compare it with the articulation they could observe in the bones they knew so well. Many a slight adjustment, often down to individual degrees of movement between vertebrae or limb bones, went into the making of the final sequences.

As the animation process entered the next phase, the creatures began to interact with one another within the waters of the Late Cretaceous. The modeled characters were digitally integrated into the film footage shot in the Bahamas, giving them a realistic underwater environment in which to swim. Weekly conference calls and meetings were set up to review each animated sequence, making sure that movements were accurate, anatomically possible, and convincing. The creatures had to move in three dimensions underwater, not just right or left, forwards and back, but up and down and in 360° of motion.

The artists and paleontologists went through many rounds of edits and revisions to the characters, making sure to correct any interpretive errors. Some of the animals were relatively easy to generate as animations satisfactory to artist and experts alike. Others were not. Many of these more difficult creatures had never been re-created accurately before. Some of the creatures, like the primitive swordfish called *Protosphyraena*, were based on recent discoveries and had never been seen before they appeared in the film. A number of others existed only as two-dimensional line drawings, created by scientists on the basis of their fossil discoveries. Envisioning them as real, live creatures presented a unique challenge because the creative and scientific teams were starting from scratch.

The hard work began to pay off as realistic views of creatures emerged in the place of long-dead skeletons. The meticulous attention to detail rendered creatures that could fascinate audiences while standing up to scientific scrutiny. Every member of the team, from the scriptwriters to the animators, the scientists, and the production crew were all dedicated to making a film that showed accurately, to the best of everyone's knowledge, how these animals really looked as they lived in Earth's marine environment 82 million years ago. Through time and teamwork, these creatures came back to life for a 21st-century audience.

TYLOSAUR STRIKE I
After an initial strike, the tylosaur seizes a shark in its mouth.

TYLOSAUR STRIKE II
The tylosaur's jaws grip the shark but do not tear its flesh.

TYLOSAUR STRIKE III
The shark is maneuvered into position to be swallowed whole.

GLASSES ON

Ghostly jellyfish float in the waters of the Late Cretaceous much as they do today. Fossils of these creatures are rare because their soft bodies decomposed quickly after death.

W HEN THE WESTERN INTERIOR SEA was formed, the Earth was much warmer than it is today. The low-lying areas of North America were inundated from the Gulf of Mexico, up through Canada, and farther north to the Arctic Circle. There were no polar ice caps on Earth, and the planet's sea levels were the highest they've ever been. The Western Interior Sea itself was no more than 600 feet deep at its lowest levels but stretched for hundreds of miles. It was home not only to large marine reptiles but also to a wide variety of other beautiful and wondrous creatures, like the large 13-foot-long *Xiphactinus* fish, opposite, to the *Caproberyx* fish and ammonites, above.

A Tusoteuthis *glides gracefully through a school of fish. Fossilized fragments of this kind of giant squid are fairly common in the Kansas chalk, but complete specimens are rare.*

GLASSES OFF
FOR NEXT PAGE

INDEX

Everhart, Mike 163, 166–167, 171, 172
Evolution, theory of 59, 64

Fick Fossil and History Museum, Oakley,
	Kans. 77, 173
Fishes 35, 93, 96; *see also Enchodus; Gillicus;*
	Sharks; *Xiphactinus*
Foraminifers 143
Fort Harker, Kans. 63, 64, 74
Fort Hays, Kans. 63, **105**
Fort Riley, Kans. 63
Fort Wallace, Kans. 49, 50, 63, 104, 107;
	soldiers 52, **107**

Galeocerdo cuvieri, see Tiger shark
Germany: fossil discoveries 18, 24, 62; muse-
	ums 72; placodont **164–165**
Giant squid 14, 91, 92, **184–185**
Gillicus: remains found inside larger fish **50–51,**
	71, 77
Gillicus arcuatus 77, **91**
Gilmore, Charles 76–77
Ginsu sharks 71–72, **84–85,** 90–91, 96–97,
	103, 113, 121; extinction 97, 121; painting
	174; predation of turtles 99; teeth 72, 90,
	96–97, **150–155**
"Godzilla" *see Dakosaurus andiensis*
Goldfuss, August 62
Gorgosaurus 42, **134**
Great white sharks 38, 72, 96, 121, 133, 153
Greek myth 26
Guizhou Province, China 15

Hainosaurs: name meaning 20
Hainosaurus 24
Hawkins, Benjamin W. 177
Hawksbill turtle **148**
Henderson, Doug 177; painting by **175**
Henodus **30, 64–65**
Hesperornis 90, 92–93, 120, **124,** 173; diving **93**
Hesperornis regalis **74,** 74–75, 92
Hoffmann, J. L. 50, 57–58
Hydrothermal vent **22**

Ichthyosaurs 14–15, **16–17,** 18, 24, 25, 30,
	101; evolution 18, 25, 31; extinction
	18, 30, 31, 98, 113, 135; fossils **12–13,**
	14–15, 17, 51, 58, 59, **144;** giant species
	15, 18, 24, 25; live birth of young 18;
	name meaning 15, 20; *see also Temn-
	odontosaurus*
Ichthyosaurus communis: drawing **176**
Institute of Vertebrate Paleontology and
	Paleoanthropology, Beijing, China: women
	measuring ichthyosaur **12–13**
Invertebrates 91–92, 99, 109, 143, 144; cri-
	noids 91, **91;** evolution 24, 25; limpets 120;
	role in food chain 141; scavenging role 53,

56; *see also* Cephalopods; Jellyfish
Iridium: rock layer **140**

Japan: fossil discoveries 15, 147
Jellyfish 38, 99, 149, **180–181**
Journey to the Center of the Earth (Verne) 15
Jurassic period 39; 19th-century painting **175;**
	sea monster evolution 12, 18, 24, 30, 118

Kansas: fossil discoveries 19, 20, 154, 163,
	167, 170; making of *Sea Monsters* movie
	156–157, 161, 167, 170–171; *see also*
	Fick Fossil and History Museum; Fort
	Harker; Fort Hays; Fort Riley; Fort Wal-
	lace; Logan County; Monument Rocks;
	Smoky Hill Chalk; Sternberg Museum
Kansas Pacific Railroad **105**
Keichousaurus hui: fossils **15**
Killer whales 15, 102, 133
Komodo dragons 58, **58**
Kronosaurs: name meaning 20
Kronosaurus 18, **162**
Kronosaurus queenslandicus 13, 19
KT boundary 135, 137, 138

Lakota Sioux legends 26
Late Cretaceous period: early water birds 92–93;
	Earth during 32–44, 134, 140–141; extinc-
	tion theories 134–149; fish 93, 96; inver-
	tebrates 91–91; marine turtles 97–99, 149;
	mosasaurs 113, 118–121, 163, 166–167;
	plesiosaurs 99–103, 108–113, 163, 166–167;
	sharks 96–96, 153
Leatherback turtles 19, 97, 98, 149
Legendary creatures 14, 26, 29
Leidy, Joseph 104, **106,** 107
Lewis and Clark expedition: fossil find (1804)
	21, 59
Liopleurodon 12, 18
Loch Ness, Scotland 26, 29; carcass on shore
	27; fossilized vertebrae **29;** legendary creature
	26, **27,** 29
Logan County, Kans.: fossil collecting **60, 61;**
	fossil discoveries 51, 74, 75, 108
Loggerhead turtles 19, 97
Lyme Regis, England: fossil discovery 50, 53, 58

Maastricht, Netherlands: fossil discovery 21,
	50, 56
MacNab, Peter 29
Maps, antique 14, **132–133**
Marine reptiles: early fossil record 19; evolu-
	tion of sea monsters 12–13, 24–25, 30–32;
	largest ever 12, 18; modern sea monsters
	26–29, 132–133; paintings **174–177;**
	"sightings" of sea monsters 11, 14, 26, 29;
	see also Ichthyosaurs; Marine turtles; Mosa-
	saurs; Plesiosaurs

ILLUSTRATIONS

All images are © 2007 NGHT, Inc. except for the following:
1, DAMN FX; 8-9, DAMN FX; 10, DAMN FX; 12-13, O. Louis Mazzatenta; 15, O. Louis Mazzatenta; 16-17, Pandromeda/DAMN FX; 18, South Australian Museum; 20-21, James R. Garvey/Emporia State University; 22, Cousteau Society/The Image Bank/Getty Images; 23, Christopher R. Scotese, Paleomap Project; 24, Sternberg Museum; 26-27, Matte FX/NGM Art; 27 (UP RT), Vo Trung Dung/CORBIS; 27 (UP LE), Bettmann/CORBIS; 27 (LO), AP/Top Foto/ The Image Works; 28-29, Matte FX/NGM Art; 29 (UP), Bettmann/CORBIS; 29 (LO), Reuters/ CORBIS; 31, Peabody Museum of Natural History; 34, Richard Lewis/Dorling Kindersley/Getty Images; 35, Douglas Henderson; 38-39, Matte FX/NGM Art; 50-51, Mark Thiessen/National Geographic Giant Screen Films; 52, Mark Thiessen/National Geographic Giant Screen Films.; 53, Natural History Museum, London; 58-59, Natural History Museum, London; 58, Brand X Pictures/ Alamy Ltd; 60, FHSU-Forsyth Library; 61 all, FHSU-Forsyth Library; 62, FHSU-Forsyth Library; 64-65, Mark Thiessen/National Geographic Giant Screen Films; 64, FHSU-Forsyth Library; 65 all, FHSU-Forsyth Library; 66-67, Mark Thiessen/National Geographic Giant Screen Films; 66 (UP), FHSU-Forsyth Library; 66 (LO), FHSU-Forsyth Library; 67, FHSU-Forsyth Library; 69, Albert J. Copley/Visuals Unlimited; 70, Mark Thiessen/National Geographic Giant Screen Films; 72, FHSU-Forsyth Library; 75, Mark Thiessen/National Geographic Giant Screen Films; 84-85, Matte FX/NGM Art; 91 (LO), Colin Keates/Dorling Kindersley; 101, Rocky Mountain Dinosaur Resource Center; 104-105 (Background), Grzegorz Slemp/Shutterstock; 104-105 (UP), Ewell Sale Stewart Library, The Academy of Natural Sciences of Philadelphia; 104-105 (LO), Ewell Sale Stewart Library, The Academy of Natural Sciences of Philadelphia; 105 (LO), Alexander Gardner, courtesy of the Kansas State Historical Society; 106-107 (Background), Grzegorz Slemp/Shutterstock; 106 (UP), Ewell Sale Stewart Library, The Academy of Natural Sciences of Philadelphia; 106 (LO LE), Ewell Sale Stewart Library, The Academy of Natural Sciences of Philadelphia; 106 (CTR RT), Peabody Museum of Natural History; 107, The Beinecke Rare Book and Manuscript Library; 112, John Sibbick/Natural History Museum, London; 113, Rocky Mountain Dinosaur Resource Center; 116, Philip D. Gingerich; 117 (UP), Robert Clark; 117 (UP CTR), Frank Greenaway/ Dorling Kindersley/Courtesy of the University of Zoology, Cambridge; 117 (LO CTR), Philip D. Gingerich; 117 (LO), Philip D. Gingerich; 118, Colin Keates/Dorling Kindersley/Courtesy of the Natural History Museum, London; 120-121, Rocky Mountain Dinosaur Resource Center; 132-133, From the collection of the James Ford Bell Library, University of Minnesota; 135, Douglas Henderson; 136-137, Douglas Henderson; 138, D. van Ravenswaay/Photo Researchers, Inc.; 139 (UP), D. van Ravenswaay/Photo Researchers, Inc.; 139 (UP CTR), NASA/JPL-Caltech; 139 (LO CTR), Mark Pilkington/Geological Survey of Canada/Photo Researchers, Inc.; 139 (LO), Dr. David Kring/Photo Researchers, Inc.; 140, Tom Bean; 142, Douglas Henderson; 144 (UP), Rolex Awards/Tomas Bertelsen; 145 (UP LE), Rolex Awards/Tomas Bertelsen; 145 (UP RT), Rolex Awards/Tomas Bertelsen; 147 (UP), Mike Everhart; 147 (LO), Pamela Everhart; 148, Karen Varndell/Alamy Ltd; 149, Gary Staab/Lair Group Inc./NGM Art/DAMN FX; 156-157, Mark Thiessen/National Geographic Giant Screen Films; 158, DAMN FX; 160-161, Ira Block/National Geographic Giant Screen Films; 162, Gary Staab/Lair Group Inc./NGM Art/DAMN FX; 163, Matte FX; 164-165, Jeffery Sangalli; 166, FHSU-Forsyth Library; 170, Mark Thiessen/National Geographic Giant Screen Films; 171, Mark Thiessen/National Geographic Giant Screen Films; 172-173, Ira Block/National Geographic Giant Screen Films; 174, Dan Varner; 175 (CTR), Duria antiquior (Ancient Dorset) depicting a imaginative reconstruction of the life of the Jurassic seas, engraved by George Scharf (1820-95) printed by Charles Joseph Hullmandel (1789-1850) (engraving) by Henry Thomas De La Beche (1796-1855) (after) © Oxford University Museum of Natural History, UK/The Bridgeman Art Library; 175 (LO), Douglas Henderson; 176 (UP), Fox Photos/Getty Images; 176 (CTR), Raul Martin; 176 (LO), Julius Csotonyi.

ACKNOWLEDGMENTS

While there are many people I would like to acknowledge for their part in making this book possible, it was my initial contacts in 2001 with Angela Botzer and John Bredar of National Geographic whose interest in my favorite subject and help along the way is very much appreciated. Associate producer Erica Meehan followed up and kept the project rolling along, while my editor, Amy Briggs, provided the leadership that turned my words into a book. Photo editor Kris Hanneman assembled an informative collection of images, while art director Melissa Farris put it all together. I also thank my co-consultants, Kenneth Carpenter and Glenn Storrs, for our informative discussions. I think the three of us would agree that it was a useful and exciting learning experience to be able to put flesh back on the bones and bring a semblance of life to these wonderful creatures: the real sea monsters. What you see in the movie and this book are the results of a lot of good people working together. I'm very pleased to have been a part of this project.

—Mike Everhart

SEA MONSTERS:
PREHISTORIC CREATURES
OF THE DEEP
by Mike Everhart

Published by the National Geographic Society

John M. Fahey, Jr., *President and Chief Executive Officer*

Gilbert M. Grosvenor, *Chairman of the Board*

Nina D. Hoffman, *Executive Vice President;*
  President, Book Publishing Group

Prepared by the Book Division

Kevin Mulroy, *Senior Vice President and Publisher*

Leah Bendavid-Val, *Director of Photography Publishing*
  and Illustrations

Marianne R. Koszorus, *Director of Design*

Barbara Brownell Grogan, *Executive Editor*

Elizabeth Newhouse, *Director of Travel Publishing*

Carl Mehler, *Director of Maps*

Staff for this Book

Amy Briggs, *Editor*

Susan Tyler Hitchcock, *Text Editor*

Kris Hanneman, *Illustrations Editor*

Melissa Farris, *Art Director*

Sanaa Akkach, *Designer*

Cameron Zotter, *Design Specialist*

Dan O'Toole, *Researcher*

Lewis Bassford, *Production Project Manager*

Marshall Kiker, *Illustrations Specialist*

Jennifer A. Thornton, *Managing Editor*

Gary Colbert, *Production Director*

Manufacturing and Quality Management

Christopher A. Liedel, *Chief Financial Officer*

Phillip L. Schlosser, *Vice President*

John T. Dunn, *Technical Director*

Chris Brown, *Director*

Maryclare Tracy, *Manager*

Nicole Elliott, *Manager*

Founded in 1888, the National Geographic Society is one of the largest nonprofit scientific and educational organizations in the world. It reaches more than 285 million people worldwide each month through its official journal, NATIONAL GEOGRAPHIC, and its four other magazines; the National Geographic Channel; television documentaries; radio programs; films; books; videos and DVDs; maps; and interactive media. National Geographic has funded more than 8,000 scientific research projects and supports an education program combating geographic illiteracy.

For more information, please call 1-800-NGS LINE (647-5463) or write to the following address:

NATIONAL GEOGRAPHIC SOCIETY
1145 17th Street N.W.
Washington, D.C. 20036-4688 U.S.A.

Visit us online at www.nationalgeographic.com/books

For information about special discounts for bulk purchases, please contact National Geographic Books Special Sales: ngspecsales@ngs.org

For rights or permissions inquiries, please contact National Geographic Books Subsidiary Rights: ngbookrights@ngs.org

SEA MONSTERS: A PREHISTORIC ADVENTURE
Motion picture copyright © MMVII, NGHT, Inc.

Funded in part by the National Science Foundation. This material is based in part upon work supported by the National Science Foundation under Grant No. ESI-0514981. Any opinions, findings, and conclusions or recommendations expressed in this material are those of the author and do not necessarily reflect the views of the National Science Foundation.

Library of Congress Cataloging-in-Publication Data

Everhart, Michael J.
  Sea monsters : prehistoric creatures of the deep / by Michael Everhart.
    p. cm.
  Includes index.
  ISBN 978-1-4262-0085-4
  1. Marine animals, Fossil. 2. Paleontology--Cretaceous. I. Title.
QE766.E894 2007
567.9'37--dc22
                              2007018671

ISBN: 978-1-4262-0085-4
Printed in the U.S.A.